THE DIA █████████ █
SOUTHPORT MAN
Paul Bagshaw

with best wishes,
Paul Bagshaw

Artworks

2002

First published in 2002
by Artworks
46 Lyndhurst Road, Southport PR8 4JT.
www.artworks-pictures.co.uk

Printed by Mitchell & Wright Printers Limited,
Banastre Road, Southport PR8 5AL.
All rights reserved

ISBN 0 9541592 1 7

Acknowledgements to:
John Lydon, Mick Mullaney, Peter Fleetwood, David Tarpey,
Fred Fouracre, Peter Forshaw, Vincent Kirk, Paul Doherty,
Robin Higham, Kenneth Hindley, Peter Simpson, Peter Hurst,
Barbara Warren, Tony Hilton, Brian Lewis, Geoff Wright Snr,
Bernard McNulty, Geoffrey Shryhane, Godfrey Hand,
Geoff Wright Jnr, Chris Riordan, Kevin Brewder,
J Arthur Dixon, Ness Studios, Ron Johns, Geoff Kean,
The Wigan Observer for photographs,
The Museo Reina Sofia in Madrid,
to Andrew Farthing of Southport Reference Library,
and thanks to Peter Ravenscroft and David Town
for their considerable help in proof reading.

by the same author:
THE DIARY OF A SOUTHPORT BOY
ISBN 0 9541592 0 9
published by Artworks in 2001

THE DIARY OF A SOUTHPORT MAN
Paul Bagshaw

CONTENTS

PART THREE
WHAT'S LOVE GOT TO DO WITH IT?
1967-69

PART FOUR
JOURNEY TO A FOREIGN LAND
1969-71

INTRODUCTION

Book One, 'The Diary of a Southport Boy', was unplanned. The idea grew from the acquisition of a laptop computer, rather from an initial urge to write. Once started, the project generated its own momentum, and the process of remembering one experience triggered the release of others which might otherwise have lain undisturbed. These must be recorded at once, for only a few hours later, they will return to the distant memory cell from where they escaped. Already, some of my errors have been spotted, but memory lapses are part of being elderly, aren't they?

In a number of ways, this second diary is less light-hearted than the first, probably because a story describing the sighting of Adolf Hitler on the number 14 bus at the age of two and a half is more engaging than an account of the anxiety felt on the first day of a new job in teaching. Whilst most stories in the first book were based in Southport, many of those in this one occur elsewhere, albeit only half an hour's drive away. It is hoped that those who were in their twenties in the 1960s will identify with some of the experiences described. It is always difficult to strike the right balance when relating anecdotes from a teaching career. Quite aside from the need for confidentiality, there is the risk of exploiting idiosyncratic behaviour of young people, simply in order to amuse. I trust that my great respect for them runs through the descriptions, for it is most sincerely felt.

The main period of time covered here is the 1960s. There are those who say that this decade has been romanticised and over-rated. Don't believe them! It was pulsating, colourful, rapidly developing and, above all, liberating...at least, for those young adults who were receptive enough to welcome change rather than to fear it. It was also a time of optimism and of confidence, although it should be admitted that some of it proved to be misplaced. This was a time to cherish, most particularly in contrast to the less positive and more cynical attitudes to life that have gained ground steadily since then, and which began to infiltrate our perceptions even before that decade had ended. The smile has been wiped from the faces of far too many in 2002, despite the fact that, for most in this country, there are still more causes to rejoice than to lament. We have become difficult to please, quicker to complain and ever more ready to blame. It is my view that the burdens most of us carry are relatively small when compared with those borne by humanity's real victims. So smile!

'I wept because I had no shoes
until I met a man who had no feet'

Paul Bagshaw

5

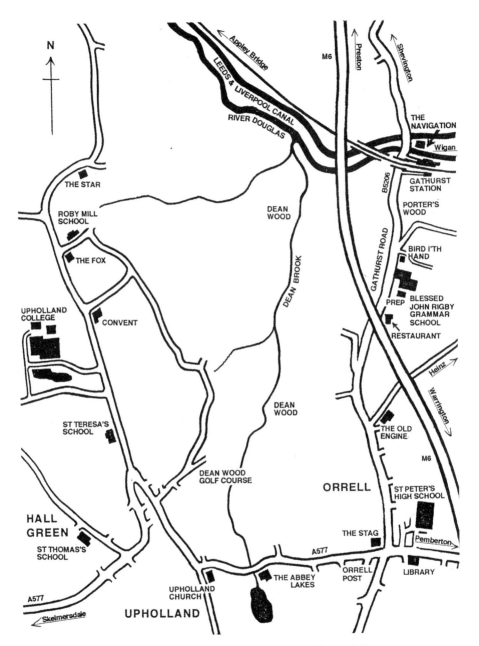

ORRELL & DISTRICT IN THE 1960s

PART ONE

HELLO, MR CHIPS
1960-62

THE SUMMER OF OUR CONTENT
THRESHOLD OF THE NEW
COLLEGIAL CHARACTERISTICS
BURNHAM
PORTRAIT OF A NARROW ESCAPE
LEARNING CURVE
EN VACANCES
A WINDFALL FROM THE FAMILY TREE
ONLY A GAME
RU18?
POST-PRODUCTION
MAST....AS ON BOARD SHIP
PARADISE MISLAID
ONWARD AND UPWARD
SHOCK OF THE NEW

1960196019601960196019601960196019601960

THE SUMMER OF OUR CONTENT

1960 was an exciting year in so many ways. For me it marked the end of boyhood, in the sense that you are not really an adult until you start earning, and this was to be my first taste of full-time work as a teacher. The end of the year saw the election of a young American President in the person of John F Kennedy, who exhorted his compatriots to be proactive by telling them *"My fellow Americans, ask not what your country can do for you; ask what you can do for your country."* He conveyed the belief that youth possessed a status and power of its own, rather than serving as a passage between inexperience and full maturity. In Britain, the transition between the teenager and the adult was no longer interrupted by National Service conscription, and so young men and women were able to mature at their own pace.

This was the year when our Prime Minister, Harold Macmillan, warned the world of a 'Wind of Change blowing through Africa', and Lonnie Donegan made a slightly less erudite contribution to contemporary thinking by getting into the charts with 'My Old Man's A Dustman'. Coronation Street started, the musical 'Oliver' opened in the West End and, although nobody realised the significance, the Beatles went on tour in

Hamburg. It was also the year of the release of Alfred Hitchcock's film, 'Psycho', after which it was rumoured that at least half of the women in the USA refused to take a shower for at least three months, an ordeal that British pre-adolescent boys had been refusing for decades.

The end of student days marked a parting of the ways for our group of friends. Brian Lewis started his National Service at the end of the NDD course and, by this time, was about halfway through his posting in Germany with the RAF. Stan Roberts had joined the firm of his future father-in-law, Eric Hutchinson, and was climbing what turned out to be a most successful business ladder. Tradge was off to Canada to start a fruitful career in graphic design, and Don Holt was about to begin the ATD course that I had just completed. My cousin, John Howells, was in the middle of a BSc course in Dairy Technology at Reading University, and Phil McLean, having graduated in French from Keble College, Oxford was working for the Reed Paper Group in Disley.

My teaching post in a Grammar School - that I had been told was probably beyond my reach as a probationer - had now been confirmed by letter. With John Mockett, my new friend and kindred spirit from the ATD course at Liverpool, I toasted our success in pints of bitter in the Grey Horse on Wigan Lane, Heath Charnock, near John's home town of Adlington. His post was at the Cardinal Allen RC Grammar School in West Derby, Liverpool, whilst mine was at the Blessed John Rigby RC Grammar School, Orrell. Comprehensive education, to which we were both attracted later, was in its infancy and, given the choice between working in grammar or in secondary modern schools, we aimed for the former, most probably for the dubious reason, if I am honest, that we thought it carried higher status and greater prospects for promotion. It was also a culture with which John and I, as former grammar school boys, were quite familiar.

Brother Ambrose, my new Headmaster, invited me to visit John Rigby before the end of the summer term and, in particular to attend a performance of 'The Bohemian Girl', the School's musical production. I enjoyed my visit, which made me feel part of the staff even before my career there began, but the performance of the 'Opera' succeeded in resurrecting those unpleasant memories, so common in the 1950s, of young boys being forced into dresses for the playing of mature female roles. Doubtless, in about ten years time, they all would enthusiastically don similar garb whilst attending drunken fancy-dress parties, but that is the young male's irresistible rite of passage. Twelve months later, I was to hear the least feminine boy in the entire school, playing the unlikely part of a princess in the production of 'Aladdin and Out', deliver the lines: 'What a terrible thing it is tu luv anibodeh. Yew are always on tenterukes, wundrin' what may 'appen tu them!'

8

There was much planning to do, and John and I made a number of visits to each other's departments before term started in order to help with the general organising of the rooms and their contents. This sharing enhanced our sense of excitement at the prospect of new and stimulating careers in a profession for which we both had unlimited enthusiasm, despite being well aware of inevitable difficulties we would have to face, particularly in that first year. Those visits to John Rigby during the summer holidays caused some alarm to the caretaker, Joe Greaves, who greeted our regular arrival at the school on these inconvenient occasions for furniture-moving purposes, with undisguised dismay. "Oh.....it's you again, Mr Bagshaw." Joe was a gentle man and a good Christian, but he clearly found it difficult to conceal his alarm at the periodic reorganising we conducted in the Art Department during this, and many other, school breaks.

Large amounts of time were spent in both departments laying out equipment, labelling items, colour-coding files, organising stock, producing visual aids and, above all, making lists. Lists had fascinated me since I had been about 11 years old, and it simply required a transference of system from the train-spotting and table football lists of the early 1950s to the Art Department procedures of ten years later. There are several who claim that preoccupation with the making of lists is a form of displacement therapy, and they are probably correct. I am certainly of the belief that listing tasks is tantamount to accomplishing them, and also that *feeling* organised is halfway to *being* organised. That is why I am a nerd, and I must admit that both my niece, Susan, and my grand-nephew, Ben, have been infected with the same obsessional virus.

John Mockett and I had similar views about what the subject of Art should offer intelligent young people. It was our belief that, just as the aim of music education is not to simply train young musicians, but rather to give a general lifelong interest in music to as wide a group as possible, the visual arts, we reasoned, should provide more than training in executive skill - how to draw, how to paint, and so on. The process of understanding is often best assimilated by 'doing', and so we devised courses in the History of Art which enabled boys to learn, for example, about Byzantine Art by making mosaics, or about Fauvism by painting Fauve versions of the landscape viewed through the art room window. Thus, when they matured and, in almost all cases, stopped painting pictures or producing sculpture, they would be left with a broad understanding and, with luck, an enriching appreciation of the visual arts. This would have a sense of permanence in that, just as we never forget how to swim or to ride a bicycle or to catch a cricket ball, so we never lose the capability to respond to the arts, once it has been acquired. Some might say that, at twenty-two years of age, both of us should have been chasing women or plotting the downfall of the government instead of becoming enthralled with matters of pedagogy. Our answer would be that, with barely two weeks to go before the beginning of our new careers, we really had no choice. We were both idealists and optimists, but the unavoidable facing of reality was almost upon us. As Elvis Presley sang at the end of 1960, 'It's Now Or Never'.

THRESHOLD OF THE NEW

I woke early from a disturbed sleep. It was 6 am. Much of the night had been filled with the anticipation and imaginings of the first day of my teaching career at the John Rigby RC Grammar School at Orrell. My half-awake mind had pored over and over the expectations of the next day. I took the bus from Guildford Road to Eastbank Street, walked to Chapel Street Station and waited for the 7.53 stopping train to Wigan. I was unnecessarily early onto the platform, and so I consumed half of the breakfast I had been unable to stomach at home. I bought a newspaper, but was too preoccupied with the thoughts of what my day might bring to bother reading it. I carried a new briefcase, very much as a five-year-old child starting at infant school would sport a new schoolbag.

This was a period when train travel was generally widespread, although the writing was on the wall as far as steam power was concerned, much to my disappointment as a former train spotter. It was still possible to travel from Southport to Preston by train out of a station that boasted 11 platforms - or 13 if you count the London Street excursion platforms. Travel to Wigan was either on the Manchester Express, which called at St Lukes, Wigan Wallgate, Manchester Victoria, or on the train that called at every station from Southport to Wigan. This one had the advantage for me that I could either alight at Gathurst or go through to Wigan Wallgate, with its large hoarding for Santus Uncle Joe's Mint Balls, and then take the School Bus to John Rigby. Whatever my choice, the charge was about 4/6d.

Dirty carriage windows and lumpy upholstery were quite normal in the early 1960s, as were the leaking cylinder drains of the 2-6-2 tank engine that pulled us. I began to realise that I did not want the journey to be over too quickly. My hands were sweating, which puzzled me because I had convinced myself that I was really looking forward to the day. My stomach was churning. What the hell was the matter with me? Why did the two others in the compartment appear so relaxed? It reminded me of those summer days in the examination hall at KGV when someone laughing in the corridor outside annoyed me intensely. How dare they even think of laughing when I was undergoing intellectual torture?

The strange mixture of eager anticipation and nervous tension was to confront me on quite a few occasions throughout my time in teaching, most

10

often when I was facing new challenges. These would consist mainly of those situations experienced for the first time: the first lesson, the first school trip, taking my first assembly, and speaking for the first time at a full staff meeting. The sensation was related to that confronting the actor, apprehensive before the stage performance, yet exhilarated by it. Most performers acknowledge the extra edge given to the quality of their work by this very anxiety, a feeling teachers know well.

I stared out through the grimy window, unfocussed on the passing landscape. Perhaps it would help if I finished my half-eaten breakfast or tried to read the newspaper. Everything else seemed unimportant compared with present concerns. At each of the stops, a member of British Railways staff would shout the name of the station in clipped 'lanky' as part of a strange litany - "Sent Lewks! Bescalairne! Busscobridge! 'Osca! Paaahbuld!" All these names became imprinted on the mind in the same manner as the daily-repeated areas of the weather forecast - Wight, Portland, Plymouth, Lundy, and so on.

When the train stopped at Parbold, two boys in grey suits and red caps entered my compartment. The undefined panic I had undergone since leaving Southport began to fade. Here in the carriage were two of my future charges, although they didn't know it yet. I concluded that they, too, were anticipating their first day at John Rigby, and listening to their excited conversation diverted me from my own fear of the unknown. They were much less anxious than I was. It was now time to pull myself together and to display an air of relaxed confidence. After all, I was a teacher - not a student teacher. Three more boys, slightly older, joined the train at Appley Bridge and, within five minutes, we arrived at our destination. "Gathust fer Shevinton!" shouted the railwayman. Gathurst Station was situated in a small wooded valley, where the River Douglas and the Leeds-Liverpool Canal ran parallel with the railway, behind which was the Navigation Pub. The five of us walked one behind another along the station approach and up the narrow pavement of Gathurst Hill in the clear morning sunshine. Just past the Bird I'th Hand Pub, managed by Jimmy Worswick, was the modern glass structure of the John Rigby Grammar School, shining blue and white in the Autumn sun.

There were four teachers new to the School staff in September 1960 - Tom Walsh, Head of English, Tony Curran, a modern linguist, Harry Finch, a Geographer, and myself. We were made most welcome in the staff room by those who had started when the school opened twelve months previously. Every school day began with a full assembly, and we entered the Hall at the back, walking behind Brother Ambrose, the Headmaster, and taking up our positions at the rear of the stage. In front of us in the assembly hall were 220 boys aged 11 to 14, all in a grey suits with red, pale

11

blue and silver badges bearing the motto 'Christo Laudes' under the shield on their breast pockets. All but the eldest wore short trousers, as was customary in the early sixties. None of them moved; the silence was complete, and every eye in this male gathering was fixed on the Head.

We all sang the rather uninspiring hymn, 'Sweet Heart of Jesus', led without piano accompaniment by Brother Gleeson, who taught both Music and Latin and who was responsible, in every sense of the word, for the School's musical productions. The pitch quality and output volume of the singing varied in inverse proportion to the boys' ages, a pattern that prevailed in all assemblies as long as I was at the school. After a short reading, a prayer, and several general announcements about the day's lunch arrangements, the staff were allowed to leave in order to prepare for the arrival of boys in their forms and for the planning of the day, whilst Brother Ambrose kept everyone else in the assembly for a 'state of the nation' address.

I was to be Form Master of 1M. I had received the list of their names by post in the week before the beginning of term, and I had tried to visualise the appearance of each of them as I copied it into my attendance register. It is strange how names evoke faces, which usually turn out to be completely different in reality. The form room was antiseptically clean, as always at the start of a new school year, and the smell of the floor polish was to become a sensory association with that period of my experience. After fifteen minutes, there was the sound of apprehensive eleven-year-olds outside the room, followed by a timid knock. I opened the door to behold twenty-eight faces looking at me with some uncertainty. They were new to the school, but they couldn't have known that this was also their form master's first day, and so the creeping anxiety I had suffered since leaving home that morning finally began to evaporate.

The morning was taken up with the making of lists, the recording of dates of birth and addresses, and the task, for each boy, of copying out his timetable, of writing his name, form and subject onto ten exercise books, and of labelling of his text books, which were delivered by older boys to the form room from the various departments. Questions came thick and fast about school rules, school meals, bus and train times, games kit, geometrical instruments, reports, and countless other subjects. The more nervous the boy, the more questions he asked. I was seen as knowing the answer to all enquiries and being capable of solving all problems. They listened to every word and accepted every explanation. I was just twenty-two and, on that first morning, I was perceived by those boys as omniscient. Even I realised that it couldn't last, but I intended to enjoy it whilst it did. The bell went for morning break. I had delivered my maiden speech to the House.....with no heckling.

COLLEGIAL CHARACTERISTICS

Just like those at any other place of work, the teachers at John Rigby came in a variety of forms. Four of them, who all held senior positions in the Grammar School, were Christian Brothers, and they lived in a community at Harvey House, adjoining the main building. There had been tales of brutality over the years by members of this order, especially in Ireland, and it is true that I was sent to King George V School in Southport, rather than to St Mary's College in Crosby, on the strength of rumours my mother had heard about the beating of boys there. I have to say that, from my own experience, Christian Brothers, like everybody else, varied from person to person; some being dictatorial and arrogant; others displaying kindness and sensitivity. Generalisations and stereotyping are rarely illuminating in such circumstances. Two further members of the Brotherhood worked in the John Rigby Prep School next door, the Head of which was Brother Kelly, noted for his strong discipline.

Brother Ambrose, my new boss, was a true gentleman who earned respect by his dignified bearing, rather than by an authoritarian manner. He was exceedingly patient with me, particularly on occasions when I overstepped the mark in arguing for the status of my subject, displaying the arrogance of youth. He was completely devoted to his constant companion, Pedro, who was a huge, white Pyrenean mountain dog. Pedro simply went everywhere with his master, and there was one occasion when, having been separated from Brother Ambrose, he entered the Hall during a morning assembly in search of our Headmaster. As everybody present suppressed the impulse to laugh, Pedro ambled slowly down the centre aisle, climbed the stairs arthritically, and walked noisily over to the Head, his heavy paws echoing on the hollow stage. It was rumoured that, whenever angry parents came to the School to complain - which was very rarely - Brother Ambrose would ask his secretary to show them into his study where Pedro dozed on the carpet, opening one eye if anyone entered the room. He would leave them alone with the dog for a few minutes; just long enough for the fear of imminent attack to soften them up. After that, they were always chastened and reluctant to offend.

The Deputy Head, Brother Baylor, was altogether more stern, and his style of teaching, with a History or Latin text book in one hand and a strap in the other, was clearly repressive, even for those days. Brother D'Arcy, Head of Maths, was succeeded by Brother Mulligan, who seemed to me a jolly man, but I understood that he drove his pupils quite hard, and he certainly pushed them to achieve impressive results in examinations. The fourth member of the Christian Brotherhood was Brother Gleeson, who taught Music and Latin, but it was for the former that he was best known. In the first Music lesson of the September term, First Year boys were

13

asked to sing solo to him and, according to their performance, were judged to be either 'singers' or 'non-singers' for the remainder of their school careers. Thus, anyone whose pitch was erratic was condemned to reading a book whilst his form-mates were exercising their vocal chords. The good news for the non-singers was that they were not compulsorily drafted into the performing of musicals such as 'The Bohemian Girl', 'Aladdin and Out', 'Ali Baba' and 'Maritana'. However, despite Brother Gleeson's taste in music differing considerably from my own, I must pay tribute to the hours, weeks and months of effort he expended in the bringing of these productions to the stage, and I have not forgotten the benefits I, myself, gained as a boy from participating in school performances.

Although Brother Gleeson was a strict disciplinarian of the old school tradition, there was an occasional glimpse of humanity in his dealings with boys. Before lunch began in the dining hall, he would insist on absolute silence. On a particular occasion, he heard a voice and assumed that the culprit was Robin Higham of 2A. On being accused, Higham tried to explain that he was not guilty but, because his voice had broken that very morning, Brother Gleeson interpreted the boy's croaking as deliberate insolence and punished him severely. After a number of Robin's friends testified to his innocence, it was discovered that the person who had broken the silence was Fred Bethell, Head of Modern Languages. Brother Gleeson apologised to Robin in front of the whole school, promising that, were the boy to be sent to him for any misdemeanour over the next two weeks, he would be let off any punishment. He kept his word.

The lay teachers on the staff in September 1960 were a mixture of the experienced and the novices. Stan Shepherd, as Head of Science, was the senior member of the common room. He spent a considerable amount of time telling us how things were done at Wigan Grammar School, where he had taught previously. He was an amusing raconteur and occasionally wore a fez during Science experiments to add interest to the lessons. Frank Balmer, Head of PE, was ostensibly a formidable man who was feared by younger boys, but perceived by the older ones as having a soft centre, which he had. However, this did not stop John Sharkey, son of a colleague who joined our staff two years later, from saying that he knew Frank was 90% bluff, but that it was the 10% that scared the hell out of him.

There was a famous lunch-time occasion when Frank Balmer had ordered four boys to stand to attention in the corridor for half an hour for some misdemeanour they had apparently committed. Three belonged to the school, but one of them was a delivery boy who just happened to be passing and, by chance, was wearing a grey pullover similar to the school's uniform. The poor kid was so frightened that he stood to attention without protesting, until his boss eventually discovered and rescued him.

14

Frank Balmer (left) and Harry Finch (right)

Brother Gleeson (left) and Headmaster Brother Ambrose (right)
Laurence Fairhurst (far left) was 'bitten by a rabbit' (see p.32)

15

Fred Bethell was Head of Modern Languages, and later became Senior Teacher at Christ The King High School just round the corner from where I live. His rather quiet manner masked a strong determination, which I witnessed on a school trip to Brittany when Fred told the hotelier in St Malo, Monsieur Lacroix, that his accommodation was well below the required standard, his brochure totally misleading, and that the party of 36 John Rigby boys and teachers was leaving at once to find somewhere else to stay. At this, we marched out leaving M. Lacroix open-mouthed.

Finally, there was Ozzie Waring who, as well as being my Head of Department in the first two years, was the most colourful character on the staff. Most of the joints executed by boys in his Woodwork lessons were held together by Evostik rather than by dove-tails, and no-one was ever encouraged to use a screw when a nail would do. "Eh, Roger, bash a nail in that!" he once ordered Roger Brown of 3T when part of the scenery in 'Aladdin', collapsed during a performance. New boys who attended his lesson on the first day each received one stroke of the strap on their hands, 'just to show them where they stood!', as Ozzie explained. For all that, he was neither dislikeable nor generally unkind, and I later discovered that he was a fine and loving father to his large family. Nevertheless, I ignored his suggestion that, once I became experienced, I would reduce my work-rate to something less frantic. 'You won't rush around like this, lad, when you're older and wiser.' I took no notice.

The most memorable aspects of Ozzie's character were best shown in the wartime stories he delighted in telling the older boys. He once claimed to have saved a large number of his colleagues, whilst on duty in South Africa, by catching a German bomb as it dropped, thus preventing a damaging explosion. I wasn't aware of any bombs in South Africa during World War II, but I didn't like to mention it. Another story told of how he once saved his own life in Norway by stabbing a German soldier with a frozen carrot, and another was a disgustingly detailed account of the open-air toilets they all had to dig and use in Calcutta. We worked out that, in May 1943, Ozzie was not only piloting a light aircraft in New Zealand, but was also involved in escapades in at least five other countries at the same time. Well, at least, they were good stories.

And that, along with Cecilia Lockett who taught part-time Art, Fr Kennedy the Chaplain, Pat Gregory who was the Head's Secretary, Joe Greaves the Caretaker, the Kitchen Staff - including a young girl who looked like Miss World - and the four new teachers, Tony Curran, Harry Finch, Tom Walsh and myself, comprised the staff of the John Rigby Grammar School at the beginning of its second year. In that situation, with boys no older than fourteen, a brand new building, and a peaceful country setting, John Rigby was not the only one who was blessed.

BURNHAM

It is difficult to imagine anything more boring to the reader of 2002 than the Burnham Pay Award to teachers in 1959. For historical reasons, and for no others, I list below the pay scales in £ per annum that were in operation at the beginning of my career:

1   Period of operation: 1st October 1959 to 31st March 1962.
2   Basic Scale: £520 to £1,000 per annum.
3   Annual increments on 17-year scale: 16 x £27.10.0 and 1 x £40.
4   Graduation addition: £90 plus £75 for 'good honours degree'.
5   Pre-Teaching Experience Increments: £27.10.0.
6   Special Schools and Teachers of Special Classes:
            £60 plus a further £50 for special qualifications.
7   Additional increments for Heads: from £150 to £1,485
            and Deputy Heads: from £100 to £665.
8   Heads of Dept: Grade A: £150, Grade B: £240,
            Grade C: £330, Grade D: £420.
9   Graded Posts: Scale 1: £90, Scale 2: £150, Scale 3: £210.
10 London Allowance: Minimum: £38, Maximum: £51.
    Now! That was interesting, wasn't it?

PORTRAIT OF A NARROW ESCAPE

One advantage of being art trained was that it provided me with a means of supplementing my income which, for a young teacher in the 1960s, was more or less a matter of necessity. I had the great pleasure of selling an oil painting towards the end of 1960 to Nancy Dixon, herself an amateur artist and, perhaps more significantly, the wife of my former King George V School Headmaster, Geoffrey Dixon. My visit to their Ainsdale home to deliver the picture - 'Still Life with Rubber Plant' - was the first time I had met Geoffrey since leaving KGV and, although I was made most welcome, I still felt afraid of him. I suppose that this schoolboy sense of awe made their acquisition of one of my works even more satisfying.

If I had used my common sense, I should have looked for graphic design commissions, a route I was to follow later. However, for my first freelance venture, I chose portraiture, a process I soon discovered to be strewn with difficulties, although I could not possibly have anticipated the bizarre experience surrounding my second venture into this project. My initial optimism was based on hardly any first-hand experience, for the only portrait I had produced as an art student was an unspeakably awful one of Beethoven who, it must be said, hadn't actually complained, although he would have had every right to do so, had he not been quite so busy decomposing.

17

The very first commission required me to portray the daughter of a friend of my mother. She was a girl of my own age, but not someone I had met before. My only anxiety was that whatever I did would fail to satisfy her parents. I recalled having produced a fairly competent drawing of my cousin when I was in the sixth form, but still failing to impress my aunt. 'It's a good drawing', she remarked, 'but it isn't John.' There really isn't any answer to a statement like that; at least, not one I could readily think of at the time. Despite this, I pressed ahead, and the girl made four visits to my house for one-hour sittings. After about a month, I displayed the finished oil painting for the approval of the family in their home. They were delighted, and I was careful to conceal my surprise as they praised my success in capturing their daughter's character. I returned home, £10 richer and with an increased sense of belief in the prospects for my new part-time career as a portrait painter.

The second commission, like the first, was of yet another daughter of my mother's circle of friends and work colleagues. Although the work I executed was completely uninspiring artistically, I was developing a sense of confidence in my ability to please my commissioners and everything went smoothly until the day came for me to take the finished portrait to the house in Churchtown for viewing. Only the mother was at home when I arrived, but she welcomed me warmly and invited me in. She was dressed most elegantly in a style more suited to an evening cocktail party than for the morning viewing of an oil painting, and was surrounded by the heavy odour of expensive perfume. I was persuaded to sit next to her on the settee and was offered an enormous gin and tonic, which I didn't really want at 10.30 on a Saturday morning, but thought it might appear impolite were I to refuse.

'Now then, you gifted young man, let's have a good look at what you have to offer me,' she began. I felt myself blushing at the double-entendre as I propped the portrait up against a chair on the other side of the room. 'Well, well! she exclaimed. 'You really *do* have hidden talents, don't you? Tell me more about yourself.' As she placed her hand on my knee, I suppressed a mounting sense of unease, slowly recognising that she was far more interested in me than in the painting of her daughter. I was totally unprepared for an encounter such as this. I was out of my depth. After all, it had taken me almost half my life to begin to understand girls of my own age, so what on earth did I know about women thirty-five years older? It wasn't a subject that had ever come up in conversation with my friends over a pint, so I had no precedent to follow. My panic was compounded by the fact that her husband, who could quite easily have returned at any moment, was built on the lines of Oliver Reed with a temperament to match.

The large gin and tonic, which I had downed rather speedily in an attempt to calm myself, was replenished by my hostess who then sat down even closer to me than before. I pondered on the irony that, if only the girls I'd fancied like mad over the years had been so forthcoming, I should have been spared a great amount of time-wasting and heartache. However, none of that mattered at this moment. I was trapped completely in a situation where I had no previous experience, no strategic plan, no idea of what might happen next, and no obvious escape route. Then, God moved in a mysterious way. There was someone at the front door. I had been, quite literally, saved by the bell!

LEARNING CURVE

Most of the experiences I encountered in that first term at John Rigby were positive. Classroom teaching surpassed my expectations, at least, as far as Art was concerned. A problem I had failed to anticipate was the difficulty of teaching Religious Instruction to my form every day of the week, a duty all form masters were obliged to perform. Because my own secondary education had not been at a Roman Catholic school, I found myself floundering when attempting to produce regular lessons that were both informative and interesting and, although I had not realised at the time, the Christian Brothers had assumed that I was in possession of the Archdiocesan Religious Teachers' Certificate. When this unfortunate gap in my qualifications was subsequently discovered, Frank Balmer took over Religious Instruction with my form, and I was told to enrol for a course on the teaching of religion in preparation for an examination that I would be unable to sit until the following summer. Although I was generally relieved by this change, I felt disappointed at the reduction of time spent with Form 1M who, after all, were my responsibility.

The older boys in 3A and 3T were a pleasure to teach, and their enthusiasm for everything we did was a great boost to my confidence. One of the most gratifying aspects of their commitment was the care and time many of them spent on producing stunning illustrations for their homework assignments. This Third form was made up largely from boys who had transferred from West Park Grammar School, St Helens, and had entered John Rigby in the second form in September 1959, primarily to attend a school closer to where they lived. Prior to the opening of John Rigby, Catholic boys in the Wigan area who passed the Eleven Plus chose either West Park, run by the De La Salle Order, or Thornleigh College in Bolton, under the direction of the Salesians. After three terms at John Rigby, these boys were placed in either 3A or 3T, according to their end of year examination performance. Those who joined 3A followed traditional Grammar School courses and, in particular, studied Latin.

3T was comprised of those boys who came below twenty-sixth place in the exam. The 'T' stood for Technical, for it was thought a curriculum with a higher practical content would suit these boys better than the more academic courses followed by the A Form. This rather rigid approach to streaming, typical of the educational outlook of the period, generally failed to question the validity of an examination designed to determine life-affecting decisions about the nation's 11-year-olds. Nevertheless, it was the system under which I had been well educated at King George V School in Southport and, for many boys in the Wigan area who might well have had no choice but to follow their fathers into the pits, it was a passport to a wider range of occupations than might otherwise have been available to them. Thus, Grammar Schools opened up new possibilities for bright young people from less prosperous families, although what was achieved for those who failed the Eleven Plus was quite another matter; one which would later be addressed by an incoming Labour Government.

The majority of the boys in this technical form were good-natured, anxious to learn, but not over-endowed with self-confidence. They, probably more than any others, convinced me that many of the visionary objectives I had set myself in that first year of my career were actually attainable. Looking back, I can now see that they reserved their greatest efforts for those teachers who demanded the most from them, who treated them with some respect, who thought them capable of making substantial achievements, and told them so. Quite simply, the more you expect, the more you get.

For the first two years of my career at John Rigby, we shared our accommodation with another school. St Peter's, a mixed secondary modern school, had no building of its own at that time, and was offered part of our 3-storey block as a temporary home. Break times and lunch times were staggered to avoid overcrowding, and I do not think either St Peter's or John Rigby were put to any great inconvenience. The Headteacher was Alban Smith, who later moved to St Aelred's in Newton-le-Willows, and was succeeded by Bernard McNulty, a fellow parishioner of mine at Our Lady of Lourdes, Birkdale. The only other teachers I remember were Peter Christopher, Michael McMahon, who became Head of English at John Rigby after Tom Walsh left, and an art teacher, Mary Woods, who became a colleague of mine one year later. I can recall only one of their pupils, a boy called Michael Kasasian, who was often sent on messages to John Rigby by the staff at St Peter's, principally I assume, because he was intelligent, articulate and smart. Perhaps not surprisingly, Michael transferred to John Rigby at the beginning of his third year, an example of the fallibility of Eleven Plus selection. At the same time, in September 1962, St Peter's moved to their new building further up Gathurst Road near Orrell Post.

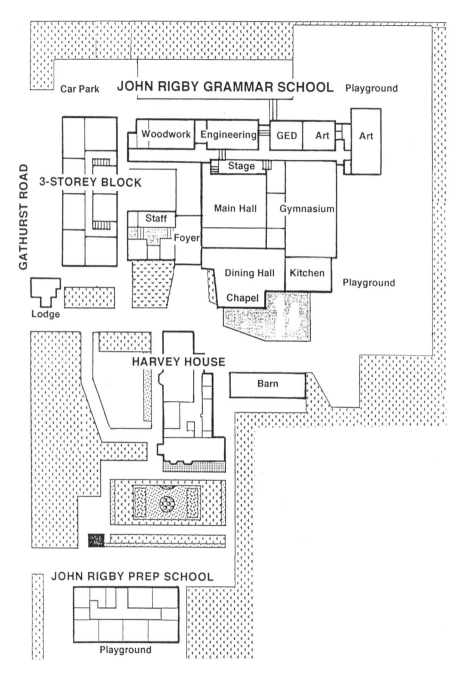

Plan of the School in 1960

EN VACANCES

By Easter, John Mockett and I decided that, in view of the massive effort we had put into our teaching responsibilities thusfar, we very much deserved a holiday and, since neither of us had any romantic relationships going at the time, we set off together for Paris. We had both studied French to A level, but John had retained far more of the language than I, and he was also studying for the Institute of Linguists examination. Hope of disguising my Englishness was dashed when we emerged from the Métro for the first time onto the Place de Clichy where I asked a passing 'Parisian' in my best gallic accent: "Pardon, monsieur. Où se trouve la Gare St Lazare, s'il vous plaît?" "Well," he replied, pointing with his umbrella, "you go down there, take the fifth road on the right, and it's facing you, old chap."

We stayed at the Hôtel d'Amsterdam near to the station. The accommodation was adequate, if not sumptuous, but we had decided that our limited money was better spent on food and wine than on hotel luxury. We found a good restaurant not far away, run by a little man called Pepe, where the steaks were good and the hospitality warm. When we returned on the second evening, he greeted us with "Allo, Meesteur Kennedee! Allo, Meesteur Rothshilde!" It was during these meals that John introduced me to Chateauneuf du Pape, still in my top five favourite wines.

Each morning we would walk down the Rue d'Amsterdam to the Place du Havre, across the Boulevard Haussmann and down to L'Eglise de la Madeleine, from which we had access to many of the finest locations in Paris. During our eight-day stay, we managed to visit a wide range of attractions, including Les Invalides, Le Musée d'Art Moderne, Le Louvre, Sainte Chapelle, Sacré-Coeur, Notre Dame and so on. It was near to the last of these that I bought a plaster cast of a charioteer as a present for my friends Stan Roberts' and Carol Hutchinson's wedding on April 15th.

We were fascinated by the Métro, and often made journeys to the end of the line, just to see what was there. One evening, a Frenchman in a bar asked us where we planned to visit the next day, and when we said we had thought of going to Montreuil, he collapsed in hysterics - Montreuil being the French equivalent of Widnes or Didcot. Because we dined well in the evening, we economised at lunch time. Our plan was to buy cheese, fruit and a cake, and to find a bench on which to sit and eat whilst watching the world go by. We disposed of any packaging by asking a passing French child to take it to the nearest litter bin, whilst rewarding him or her with a threepenny bit. I imagine that in today's world we might be arrested for holding an uninvited conversation with, as well as bribing, juveniles.

The Paris shops were wonderful, packed with goods that, to us in 1961, seemed quite exotic. The shopkeepers, however, were less agreeable and consisted mainly of middle-aged women, with boney elbows, sharp noses and stern expressions, who watched our every move. We visited a number of book shops, mainly to look at the art, but bought very little on account of the high prices. In Paris, leaving a shop without making a purchase was perceived as a grave sin, and the undisguised hostility of the proprietress was conveyed to us with an icy farewell - "Au revoir, *Messieurs!*" - as we moved towards the exit.

Our holiday ended with the rail journey to Calais and the channel crossing to Dover. John and I agreed that these ferries were the most primitive form of travel imaginable. Also, they featured the additional disadvantage of being overwhelmed with large crowds of hyperactive children returning from their French trips under the weary supervision of exhausted teachers. We would soon be joining their number when we planned our own school trips in later years, against a background of the amazing misconception that teachers take parties abroad mainly to 'get a free holiday'. They should try it!

Down in the aptly named 'smoking lounge', we drank bitter coffee as we scrutinised this strange cross-section of the human race, found only on channel boats or, nowadays, in motorway cafés. The most bizarre of these was a long-haired man in his twenties, dressed from head to foot in brown corduroy, reading a crumpled paperback book in the dim light, whilst wearing sunglasses - not so much a fellow passenger as a fellow-traveller. The holiday did us both good and refreshed us for the facing of our third term in teaching. It now seems strange to admit that this was my first time abroad, and that at the age of twenty-three!

A WINDFALL FROM THE FAMILY TREE

From the age of three I had been obsessed by cars and everything to do with them. Unfortunately, I had to wait until I was twenty-one before I owned one, and even then, I had not got as far as taking my driving test. There was no chance at all of affording driving lessons, but I was given the opportunity to gain driving experience by Marie Catlow, a friend and work colleague of my mother. Marie's main interest was in collecting antiques, and she often visited sales in Lancashire and Yorkshire in the hope of picking up bargains. Since she did not particularly enjoy driving long distances, she wondered if I would like to be her driver at weekends. What an offer! I was delighted, even though the car in question was a Morris 1000 Estate.

Over a period of several months I drove Marie to sales in various parts of the north of England, gaining much valuable experience behind the wheel, as well as confidence on the road. By March 1961, the date of my driving test came round - a landmark in the passage to full adulthood and independence. The Morris had semaphore indicators, rather than winkers, and these were operated by a switch on the dashboard. As I drove up Lord Street and indicated left to turn into Leicester Street for my test, the switch came off in my hand. As a result, I was forced to use hand signals throughout the test - not really what I would have preferred. In addition, my attempt to reverse smoothly round a corner was marred by the rear near side tyre mounting the kerb. As I brought the car to a halt, I guided the tyre ever so slowly and carefully down the edge of the kerb and gently onto the road, hoping that the instructor would not notice my mistake. "You did that so well that you almost fooled me," he said with an ironic smile. My God! I've failed! But I hadn't...I'd passed!

One morning, in May 1961, my mother received an unusual letter. It was from the Honourable Mark Watson, brother of Lord Manton, and was handwritten on prestigiously expensive notepaper with an impressive crest at the top. He told her that he was in the process of producing a family tree, and that our relatives on my father's side were to be included. He very much wanted to visit us and to learn more details of the Bagshaw family. She wrote back at once, inviting him to Lyndhurst Road to look at family photographs. So it was that a tall, distinguished man in his early sixties arrived at our house one Saturday morning to further his enquiries. He took us out for lunch at the Royal Hotel on Southport Promenade, and later for coffee in the afternoon sun in the gardens fronting Southport Town Hall. We returned to Lyndhurst Road and Mark spent the remainder of the afternoon looking at photographs with my mother, asking her about family details, and making extensive notes about members of the Hales and the Bagshaws, the former being my mother's side of the family.

The Hon. Mark Watson had been educated at Eton. He had retired from a career in the diplomatic service, during which he had been Her Majesty's Attaché in Washington from 1930 to 1932, and in Paris from 1932 to 1934. In the Second World War he had served as a Flight Lieutenant with the RAF Volunteer Reserve. He still owned a ranch in California, and his English residence at that time was at Brompton Square in West London, a magnificent five-storey dwelling, which I was to visit on several occasions subsequently. He was the youngest of four brothers, the eldest bearing the title Lord Manton, and he displayed a refined courtesy that we all expect to witness, but do not always encounter, in the behaviour of the upper classes. He seemed interested in my new career, and his good wishes for my success in the teaching profession appeared warm and genuine. It was all rather exciting, not least because the entire episode had been completely unexpected.

My 1937 Vauxhall 14

The Hon Mark Watson and my mother in Lord Street Gardens

Mark left us to return to London in the early evening, clearly most grateful for the additional information for the family tree that he had been able to gather as a result of his visit to Southport. As he walked along our drive, he asked if my car - a 1937 Vauxhall 14 six-cylinder banger bought for £30 from my fellow art student Donald Holt twelve months previously - was practical for my journey to school. It was a fair question, and I told him that I generally travelled to work by train, principally because the Vauxhall leaked oil and was very thirsty on fuel. What I failed to mention was that I could not actually afford to tax and insure the vehicle on my current teacher's salary. "You really could do with something smaller and more economical to run for your journey to school," he remarked as he bid us farewell and drove away smoothly in his automatic Austin Westminster. I nodded, but thought no more about it. Why should I?

Life returned to normal. My journeys to school alternated between those where I alighted at Gathurst and carried my marking up the hill, and those when I chose to go on to Wigan Wallgate and to take the School Bus. As far as I knew, and in view of my financial circumstances, there was no foreseeable alternative to this mode of transport. Then, a few days later I received a letter:

55 Brompton Square
London

Dear Paul,

I so much enjoyed meeting you and your mother on Saturday, and I have gained much valuable information for the family tree. I hope we may meet again soon, and you must visit me next time you are in London.

I have decided to buy you a car, because the one you have at present seems too large to be practical. Sometime at the beginning of June, a new Mini will arrive at your address, taxed and insured, from Stewart & Arden in London. I do hope that you enjoy it.

With every good wish,

Mark

I read the letter over and over, unable at first to grasp the reality of Mark's offer. Yes, he actually did say that he was buying me a car. Amid the confusion, it dawned on me that I would have to write an acknowledgement, but what an earth was I to say? After much thought, I started my letter: "Dear Mark, I really don't know how to respond to your generosity, except to say a heartfelt 'Thank You' ". I imagined that he had a number of nephews and nieces of my age, but that they were probably prosperous enough to buy their own cars. Clearly, he was a wealthy man, but not everyone with money is generous in such an unselfish way. I was quite overwhelmed by his kindness, and the excitement of anticipation was almost unbearable.

The next three weeks seemed like years as I waited for my new transport, just like a six-year-old longing for Christmas. One Thursday, at about 5.30 pm, a phone call came from Stewart & Arden announcing the delivery of a new Mini to Lyndhurst Road on the following afternoon, and asking if anyone would be at home. The train journey from Gathurst to Southport on Friday after school had the atmosphere of a film in slow motion. I scrutinised the other passengers, wondering what they were going home to. Not a new car, that's for sure. All of a sudden, I realised that I was smiling at strangers in the carriage, and I stopped at once, feeling rather foolish. So desperate was I to get home as quickly as possible that I took a taxi from Chapel Street Station, an extravagant but justifiable move. The taxi driver slowed down as he approached number 46. There, parked in the drive, was a shining mid-blue Mini, registered as 5990 MT. 'My car,' I told him. 'Two shillings,' he replied, showing not even the slightest interest in my magnificent new acquisition.

The seats of the car were neatly wrapped in polythene and there were cardboard Stewart & Arden mats on the floor, neither of which I was tempted to remove. This was the cult car of the moment - a spectacular example of British innovation - a young man's status symbol. As I edged gingerly out of the drive, one of the most seductive features of my Mini was the smell, made more appetising because I had never even sat in a new car before, let alone owned one. I drove carefully up Clifford Road, turning left into Liverpool Road, and made for the most prosperous section of Birkdale -

Waterloo Road, Selworthy Road, and so on. I desperately wanted people I knew to see me, but, as is so often the case, they were nowhere to be found. I also started the lifelong habit of parking the car and then casting backward glances at it as I walked away. Never, before or since, have I been high on drugs, but the feeling in that car on that afternoon must have come close to a psychedelic trip. The cliché, 'Life was never quite the same again', fitted perfectly.

That weekend I took a number of trips in the new car, hardly any of them really necessary. By Sunday afternoon I was running low on petrol, and so I turned into Worcester Garage at the top of our road to fill up. The attendant put five gallons into the Mini, a large order by my previous standards. I can remember the day three years previously when my fellow art student, Rob Peters, pulled into the petrol station opposite the Art School on Mornington Road and asked for a pint of Esso. The man at the pump simply served him, displaying no surprise at the minimal order. Anyway, my car received its petrol and the attendant asked if I would like the battery topping up. I agreed. "Where is it?" he asked. I smiled with an unjustified air of superiority and released the bonnet lock. It took the pair of us two minutes to establish that, wherever the battery was located, it was not at the front of the car. My complacent pose was wearing thin now, as we both conducted a search of the boot, eventually discovering the battery lurking under the floor mat. "Ah, yes, of course!" I remarked unconvincingly, utterly failing to mask my encyclopaedic ignorance of the Mini's principal parts. It was time to read the handbook.

It is almost impossible to convey the extent to which car ownership changed my life. In no time at all, I could hardly remember how on earth I had managed on public transport, and I made numerous journeys to and fro, often for no particular reason. Driving to work was superb - no waiting on draughty station platforms; no carrying of marking uphill through the drizzle; no agony caused when missing a train by two minutes. Above all, there was the panache of swinging into the school car park like a racing driver. The fact that it was a Mini took nothing away from the glamour.

As I adapted to my new means of transport, I began to delay my departure from home to the last possible minute, which caused me to be late for school several times, and resulted in my being caught in the radar speed trap - recently introduced - on three occasions in eighteen months. To add to this, I ran out of petrol about once a month, firstly because I could afford only two gallons at a time and, secondly, because I put too much trust in the accuracy of the fuel gauge. Despite all this, nothing could detract from the sheer delight of independent motoring in my own car. In 1961, Yuri Gagarin was in space and I was in my Mini. 'Halfway to Paradise', sang Billy Fury.

My new Mini at the front of the John Rigby Grammar School

John Rigby   Grammar School

ORRELL,   LANCASHIRE.

The school's first Rugby team

29

ONLY A GAME

My interest in Rugby had faded considerably since schooldays, just as my passion for soccer had increased. Now, the situation demanded a re-examination of Rugby Union. As a grammar school, John Rigby favoured the oval ball, but then so did the area from which the school drew. Most boys in Wigan, as well as in the other South Lancashire towns like St Helens, Warrington and Widnes, played Rugby League to a competent level in the Primary Schools. Such was the dedication of many that, during their free time, these boys played 'Scrog', which is Rugby on cobbled streets *with real tackling*. Given this background, eleven-year-olds arrived at John Rigby as experienced players needing only to adapt from League to Union. Thus, the School could turn out an Under 12 team capable of running rings around all other schools except those that enjoyed a comparable advantage.

In those days in most schools, such was the enthusiasm of male teachers for participating in schoolboy sport that there were more staff willing to coach teams than there were teams to coach. This was in spite of the fact that, in order to run a Rugby or Soccer team, a teacher - probably not a PE specialist - would have to give up about twenty Saturdays a year, to travel to and from the school at his own expense, to take two practices a week at either lunch time or after school, to referee and then supervise all refreshments for home games, to be responsible for the supervision and welfare of teams travelling to away fixtures, taking any injured boys to hospital when necessary and remain with them until parents arrived, and all of this without pay.

Teachers in 2002 might reflect on this before they assume that the job was dramatically easier until a few years ago. Nevertheless, it is fair to concede that, in the 1960s, we had much more discretion in choosing the kind of extra contribution we wished to make, and we were certainly spared the present-day volume of administration, as well as the intense levels of scrutiny and public accountability that operate within today's schools. Furthermore, the problem of pupil misbehaviour was not at its present level. There were signs of an emerging teenage culture as early as the beginnings of Rock 'n Roll, but it was relatively mild and certainly less impenetrable than that of today. Good committed teachers have always worked hard, but external pressures have undoubtedly seen an increase in their work load over recent years.

My earliest involvement in the coaching of Rugby came in the games lesson with First Year boys in September 1960. As Head of PE, Frank Balmer was in charge, and I learned enthusiastically from his teaching methods. His tough exterior ensured that the activity was taken very seriously by all on the pitch, and short shrift was paid to anyone failing to try his best. However, there was a discernible kindness lurking under the surface, and praise was given just often enough to retain its value. Twelve months later, I was still sharing a team with Frank, but I was taking a greater responsibility for their coaching. As the season progressed, he left me more and more often to take the lessons on my own, which boosted my confidence and, in the September of 1962, I took over the group entirely as Under 13s, having attended a Rugby coaching course at Padgate College run by the English Schools Rugby Football Union in the Summer holidays.

Coaching schoolboy sport was an absorbing and rewarding activity, but not without its difficulties. Quite early in my refereeing career, I was in charge of a home game against another Christian Brothers' School. The visiting member of staff, a Brother himself, inflicted me with a litany of lament and criticism for the first ten minutes of the match, objecting to almost everything awarded against his team and shouting criticism of my perceived failure to penalise the John Rigby team for their alleged misdemeanours. At last, I could stand this no longer, and I stopped the game, walked to the touchline, held out the whistle and offered him the opportunity to referee the remainder of the fixture. He blushed with embarrassment, declined and behaved impeccably thereafter. Perhaps I was rather stern, but at least I can claim provocation.

Another feature of coaching was the agony of watching from the touchline, unable to influence the play except by shouts of encouragement and the occasional piece of tactical advice. This was most acute in Sevens where games can be won and lost in seconds, often by an unexpected mistake from which it is too late to recover. Of course, these regular nerve-jangling experiences are what makes Rugby in particular, and sport in general, so absorbing. In that respect, it is related to the tension experienced in the performing arts where, so often, people perform at their very best when the stakes are high. In both activities, the pleasure of shared experiences, and the camaraderie they engender, explain why team sports and corporate performances prove so valuable as means of self-development.

One of the most unusual fixtures was that played against Newton Grammar School by the eldest boys at John Rigby. With one exception, the Newton-le-Willows team was moderate in ability, to say the least, and offered little in the way of opposition. The exception was a boy of powerful physique and enormous talent, and our boys tried their best to prevent him getting the ball. "Don't let that bloody mongol get hold of it!" was their cry, 'mongol' being a colloquial term for someone with Downs Syndrome. In fact, the boy in question was not at all what they thought, although his large jaw and thick neck explained the misperception. He was later to play for Lancashire, the North, England and the British Lions, and his name was Fran Cotton.

31

Just as at KGV as a boy, I found summer sport of little interest to me, although I still preferred cross-country running to cricket, given the choice. One afternoon, Frank Balmer, the Head of Physical Education, decided that everyone would go on a cross-country run around the fields at the back of the school, a distance of about two miles. All went smoothly until a small member of the Second Year, Laurence Fairhurst, returned from the run and announced that he had been attacked by an animal. There, clearly visible on his thigh, were two small teeth marks. "What sort of animal was it, Fairhurst?", Frank asked him. "Sir, a rabbit." And so, the games session came to an end with an entry in the Accident Book which read: *'Fairhurst, Laurence; Form 2B; Small wound on right thigh caused by rabbit bite; Antiseptic cream and elastoplast applied to wound; Referred to Wigan Infirmary for anti-tetanus jab'.* We thought it was a hare.

RU18?

Forty years ago, life was markedly different from what we know today, even though the changes of the Sixties were already beginning. One contrast can be seen in the price of cigarettes, then costing 1/9d (about 8p) for ten. The ending of Children's Hour on radio signalled the passing of old ways, and the launching of the E-type Jaguar heralded the new age. In September 1961, my niece and God-daughter, Susan Bagshaw, started at Southport High School for Girls, having completed her junior school education at Farnborough Road in Birkdale. By this time, the school had moved from its depressing premises in Scarisbrick New Road to attractive new buildings near to the Royal Birkdale Golf Club.

Meanwhile, I was still worried about looking youthful. Although this was not as great a concern as it had been when on teaching practice with sixth formers only three years younger than I was at Merchant Taylors School, it was at the back of my mind with Fourth Year Art groups at John Rigby. I felt the lack of a certain gravitas, and this, I considered, could not really be conveyed by a baby-faced countenance. What I needed were facial lines like those of Beethoven - a reflection of life's difficulties coupled with the strength of character to overcome them. It was a forlorn hope, of course, just as was my unfulfilled search for anger in the late 1950s.

The embarrassment of youth was not restricted to my professional career. It was also a feature of everyday life at home, most of all when I bought alcohol from Massam's off-licence on the corner of Liverpool Road and St Johns Road in Birkdale. Even when I was in my twenties, old Mrs Massam insisted upon asking me suspiciously if I was 18, despite the fact that I shopped there at least once a fortnight. Mrs M would then ask me to guess her age, before telling me hers. Here is one of the many encounters we conducted over this matter:

Me:	"Four large bottles of brown ale please, Mrs Massam."
Mrs Massam:	"Are you eighteen?"
Me: (crossly):	"Yes, I'm twenty-three."
Mrs Massam:	"I bet you can't guess how old I am."
Me:	"Er, no."
Mrs Massam:	"Go on, guess."
Me (tactfully):	"Sixty-six?"
Mrs Massam:	"No, I'm eighty-three."
Me:	"Oh."

Time after time we enacted this same dialogue, somewhat in the style of a television quiz show ritual, until I became so exasperated that I behaved in a way I now regret. A later conversation went as follows:

Me:	"Six bottles of Worthington Green Shield, please."
Mrs Massam:	"Are you eighteen?"
Me (wearily):	"Yes, I'm twenty-three."
Mrs Massam:	"I bet you can't guess how old I am."
Me:	"No."
Mrs Massam:	"Go on, guess."
Me:	"No."
Mrs Massam:	"Go on!"
Me:	"Alright....ninety-five."
Mrs M (icily):	"Will that be all?"
Me:	"Yes thank you."

It was very unkind of me I know, but at least Mrs Massam never again asked my age after that encounter. In conclusion, I really must express my strong admiration for her dedication in working well into her eighties; a fine lady indeed.

196219621962196219621962196219621962

POST-PRODUCTION

Pupils of the Blessed John Rigby Grammar School present

'ALADDIN AND OUT'

A COMIC OPERA IN THREE ACTS

June 19th to 24th 1961 at 7.15 p.m.

ALADDIN	GEOFFREY HALL
BADMANAZAR (Wicked magician)	PETER FORSHAW
WINKEY-WUM (Emperor)	STEWART CLOUSTON
PHATMAN (Prime Minister)	PETER FLEETWOOD
SO-SO (His son)	WILLIE AINSCOUGH

33

TOEDEE (Courtier)	JOHN WALMSLEY
SICK-O-FANT (Courtier)	TERRY SYKES
GENIE OF THE LAMP	ROGER BROWN
GENIE OF THE RING	MICHAEL MULLANEY
FIRST GUARD	IAN HYDE
SECOND GUARD	BRENDAN HURLEY
THIRD GUARD	LAURENCE WILSON
MRS MUSTAPHA (Aladdin's Mother)	JOHN McDERMOTT
PHULMOUN (Emperor's daughter)	GERARD HOUGHTON
BUTEA	PHILIP MORAN
BO-HEA	DANNY McNAMARA
PEEP-BO	ALFRED MOCKETT
SO-SHY	FREDDY MOSS
KANAIRI	BERNARD HEDLEY
SERAPHINA	HUGH CROOKE
FELICITY	BRENDAN McGUINNESS

At the John Rigby Grammar School, Brother Gleeson pressed on with musical productions. In 1960, it was 'The Bohemian Girl', in 1961 'Aladdin and Out', and this year 'Ali Baba'. My principal rôle in all this was that of set designer, a task I approached with enthusiasm. My aim was to provide a visual experience for the audience immediately the curtains opened, and for that I chose to present the scene as a surreal Arab townscape in bright red and white. This delighted the boys who happily volunteered to give up their lunchtimes as scenery painters, and quite clearly perplexed Brother Gleeson, whose taste in the arts was generally conservative.

The only mishap at this time occurred when a boy called Peter Woods, who was not one of the scenery painting team, decided to climb a stage ladder when no-one else was around, and continue the painting of the sky in bright vermilion. This, in itself, would not have mattered, had he not lost his grip on the ladder when descending, covering his grey uniform with red paint. His parents were understandably angry, mainly because Peter's uniform was brand new, for he had joined John Rigby only a few weeks previously. Fortunately, I was exonerated by the fact that he had acted without permission. Much worse things happened, things that I knew nothing about at the time. Peter Fleetwood told me how his form-mate Cavanagh had a rope tied around his ankles, was hoisted up on a pulley and left dangling upside-down twelve feet above the stage during one of the scenery-painting sessions

Most of the set-painting coincided with rehearsals, and so we got to know, not only the production itself, but also the musical director's techniques of getting the best out of his cast. Those who had been deemed 'non-singers' were spared participation, but all others with unbroken voices were more or less compelled to perform. The lucky ones played male parts. Those less fortunate would be inducted into the roles of giggling maidens or, even worse, busty wenches, thrust unwillingly into exotic garments made by their mothers. Throughout the process of refining the quality of the performance, Brother Gleeson took no prisoners in his quest for excellence, and woe betide the boy who sang 'a bum note' or put his parasol on the wrong shoulder. When Robin Higham's voice broke two weeks before he was due to play the Gipsy Queen, he feared for his life!

'Ali Baba' was actually a great success as far as the audience were concerned, but they were most probably unaware that most of the drama occurred backstage. Brother Baylor was stage manager, and he brought to the job a ruthless control for which he had already earned a reputation as Head of History and Deputy Head. Boys who made clumsy entrances or exits to and from the stage were 'dealt with', and anyone who talked when he should have been silent was in danger of being strapped. In the previous year's production, the wash-tubs, which had been made in the woodwork room under Ozzie Waring's low-tech supervision, started to fall apart as they were moved off the stage, at which Brother Baylor screamed at the scene-shifters, and called on Ozzie to sort the problem out forthwith. This was the origin of the command: "Bash a nail in that, Roger!", as Ozzie told Roger Brown of 3T to start the process of wash-tub repair.

The orchestra was made up of 'friends' of the school, although, in some cases, their playing was of a lower order than their friendship. It was no secret to us that Brother Gleeson, as conductor, sometimes found them exasperating, even though he was grateful for their efforts. He once remarked to me: "I knew they were all incapable o' starting together, but I thought that, at least, I would get them to finish together, and then didn't a hair o' Joe Cunningham's bow scrape across a string and go 'aaaagh!', just as the last chord was dying away." He was right. Their rendering of 'God Save The Queen' strongly resembled the anthem of a small, emerging nation greeting a dignitary from the developed world.

Despite lapses of co-ordination by the orchestra, boys forgetting their lines or, worse still, speaking someone else's lines, and Brother Baylor losing his temper backstage, it was obvious that the production was enjoyed by the audience, and everyone who took part felt pride in their achievement. By tradition, there was a gathering in the Staff Room afterwards for staff and parent helpers, governors and friends of the school, hosted by Brother Ambrose. Trays of sandwiches and cakes were devoured and large amounts of alcohol were consumed, for this was a time well before breathalysers had even been thought of.

This event was also a time for singing, and anyone who wished could sing a solo, confident of lusty support from others present. Brother Gleeson always sang 'Danny Boy', but insisted on singing in Gaelic, which prevented many of us from joining in. This would have been fine, had the

35

Michael Mullaney, Stewart Clouston, Geoffrey Hall, Robin Higham
Principals from 'The Bohemian Girl' in 1960

The surrealist red-sky set for 'Ali Baba' in 1962

words fitted the music as they did in the English version. In Brother Gleeson's rendering, there seemed to be two or three syllables too many at the end of each line. We smiled in support as he sang.

However, 'Danny Boy' was as nothing when compared with the song that followed. A young woman - the daughter of a local family (whom I shall not name) - sang 'I Could Have Danced All Night' with enormous gusto and at maximum volume. Unfortunately, she had a heavily pronounced lisp, and so the second verse - 'I could have thpread my wingth, and done a thouthand thingth' - caused me the agony of withholding pent-up laughter, a major difficulty I was to encounter on so many occasions, particularly when my friend, John Mockett, was within eyeshot, as on this occasion. There were many times when we sat next to each other at formal gatherings, such as speech days, and I would feel my chair shaking with the laughter he was deperately trying to contain. His face would be impassive, but his shoulders revealed that tell-tale vibration of mirth that dare not reveal its presence.

Despite all the ups and downs, these musical productions were well worth undertaking, and I suspect that most of the boys who took part would now look back with some satisfaction, even if the experience was something of an ordeal at the time. For me, there was a return to that relationship with performance I had valued as a boy - the corporate pride, the camaraderie, the withdrawal symptoms after the final performance, when months of work climaxed within the space of a few days.

MAST....AS ON BOARD SHIP

In Summer, John Mockett and I decided to take a holiday in Belgium and France, this time by car. Although the Mini had a restricted luggage capacity, we used the back seats for items that would not fit into the boot. Nothing eventful happened on the journey until the channel ferry approached Ostend. It was then that we were approached by a small, thin American who resembled the veteran film actor, Joe E Brown, and spoke in the relaxed manner of the comedian, Jack Benny. "Are you, by chance, going north?", he enquired. We nodded, and granted his request for a lift, although the problem of fitting one more person with his rucksack into the car was almost impossible.

"I, too, am a teacher, like yourselves," he informed us. "My subject is related to your own of Art. I am a teacher of Wood, Metal and Technical Drawing." We smiled, trying to appear engrossed by this, and asked him about teaching in the United States. "The discipline in the United States schools is just *dreadful!*", he informed us, emphasising the final word with a weary arm gesture. "It is nothing at all for a teacher to be punched into a locker by his students." We pictured this skinny man, with a huge student towering over him, pleading: "OK...show me the locker and I'll get in there, but... heck...don't punch me!"

We set off in the bulging Mini, making for Bruges. To appear helpful and sociable, our passenger read out details of our destination from his guide book in a slow and unexpressive monotone. *"Bruges is a city of one hundred and ten thousand people, and has a canal system that has earned it the title 'Venice of the north',"* he informed us. *"Notable sights include the Basilica of the Holy Blood, the historic Market Square, the Memling Museum...I guess he was a General in the Belgian Army or something like that...the Groan, er, Groon...some other museum."* "Groeninge', explained John who, with his talent for European languages, had managed to teach himself a considerable amount of Flemish (Dutch) in the three months before the holiday took place.

Our next stop was to be Ghent and, once again, we were treated to the reading of a long paragraph of statistics about the city from the guide book. It was time to eat, and so we found a restaurant and ordered steaks, which the Flemish cook in a manner agreeable to the English palate. The phone on the bar counter rang, and one of the staff answered the call, speaking in Flemish on this occasion. Our passenger was intrigued by the frequency of a particular word. He leaned over towards us and, in a low, conspiratorial whisper, asked "Tell me, is 'Ja' French for 'Yes'?" John smiled and shook his head. "Ah, I see," the American replied, "I guess it's some sort of slang."

As we returned to the car, the teacher of Wood, Metal and Technical Drawing stopped to admire a medieval wrought iron bell-pull on the door of a convent. "Just look at that," he exclaimed. "My students have made pokers just like that!" In those days, it was usual to mock the American attitude to history and culture. The truth is that, whilst they were marvelling at European cathedrals, galleries and museums, their English counterparts were searching for Kellogg's Cornflakes, tea bags and marmalade, drinking themselves into oblivion, and shouting in English at foreigners as a means of making themselves understood.

We took the concrete autoroute to Brussels and made conversation on the way. We asked our passenger how some of the American states got their names, but he didn't seem to know much about the subject. We suggested that a few of them may have been named after Indian tribes, to which he replied, "Mm...well...I guess so. Take, for instance, Indiana." The presence of these indigenous people appeared to have made no impression whatsoever upon him. "When the Europeans arrived," he said, "the Indians just folded up their tents and moved on." Sitting Bull might well have disagreed.

The hot sun, combined with the American's soporific voice, made our eyelids heavy. The first to fall asleep was our passenger and, as we sped towards the Belgian capital, John was beginning to nod. Eventually he, too, faded away and, as the only one awake, I began to feel alarmed at my own fatigue. My first bout of unconsciousness lasted for only a fraction of a second. As time went by, the duration of these lapses increased. It is now horrifying to recall that, for a period of what must have been about ten seconds, all three of us slept in a fully laden car travelling on the autoroute at sixty-five miles per hour. We were saved by the joins in the concrete road surface - most especially, one badly fitting join. At the resultant bump, all three of us awoke with a start, and found ourselves staring at a huge image in front of the car. It looked like a giant Ace of Clubs. In fact, it was the back of an enormous log wagon and, had we not been wakened when we were, we should most certainly have ploughed into the back of the vehicle, killing ourselves in the process. Mon Dieu!

As we entered Brussels, we were joking about making a sign for the back window of the Mini saying "No hand signals - occupants asleep", but our laughter at this was just a shade nervous. Our American passenger thanked us most courteously for the lift and for our companionship as he extracted his rucksack from the back seat. When we asked him what his plans were, he said he would hitch a lift to Rotterdam and hire a moped to travel over Holland. John imagined him in the centre of Rotterdam, asking himself, "Heck...what's the Dutch for moped?"

As our transatlantic friend hoisted the huge rucksack onto his frail shoulders, holding out his hand in thanks and farewell, we realised that we hadn't asked his name. "It's Mast....Ed Mast," he replied. Then, in an explanation he had probably given a hundred times, he added, "Mast...as on board ship". With this, the slightly-built American wandered off and round the corner out of sight. We looked at each other for a moment and burst out laughing, half wondering if we had imagined the entire episode. Twelve months later I received a postcard from Ed in which he described a journey of considerable distance throughout Europe over a period of two months at a cost of about $350. He was nothing if not resourceful.

John and I continued our journey, making up the route as we went along, and stopping for the night wherever we happened to be. There was one occasion in Nancy when we simply could not find two single rooms, mainly because we had left it too late, and so we decided to sleep in the Mini, John in the back and I in the front. To our surprise, we awoke to discover that we had parked and slept in the entrance to a graveyard! Another memory, relating to our love of practical jokes, was of driving into a small village, stopping the engine, and telling the locals that we had run right out of water. They had all assumed we meant petrol, but we insisted

39

otherwise, announcing that this Mini was the first car in the world to run on water. With a shrug and an expression of disbelief, a kind man brought us a large jug of water, which John used to fill up the screen washer reservoir. I then pressed the starter and the mini's engine roared into life, much to the bafflement of the small crowd of villagers. We imagined an old man going back home and telling his wife that he had just seen a car that ran on water. "Oh, Georges! You are so stupide! You 'ave been at ze Cognac againe!"

PARADISE MISLAID

On the third occasion I was caught speeding by the Police radar trap on Ormskirk Road in Hall Green, Upholland, on my irresponsibly late journey to school, I was unable to find my driving licence, and was therefore required to produce it within three days at my local constabulary. Although I was very highly organised at work, most of my personal items and documents were kept randomly in a number of drawers, cupboards and shelves at home. Once I had given up the fruitless search, I decided to visit the Vehicle Licensing Department in Southport. This was located in a dark building halfway up Post Office Avenue, off St. George's Place near the monument.

The room I required was one of several decorated in the obligatory local corporation gloom. A serviceable, but depressing, dark brown colour was on the walls up to shoulder level, then a one inch black line and, above that, regulation cream. It was gloss paint, which no doubt made it easier to clean, but most revealing of every imperfection in the plaster. On one side of the long room ran a counter with frosted glass panels above it and three openable hatches, all of which were closed. A regulator wall clock ticked relentlessly, and it was possible to make out the hazy silhouette of a corporation employee behind the glass. Cinéma-vérité, certainement!

I tapped on the glass of the nearest window. After one minute, I tapped again. The hatch was opened. "Yes?" A plump, self-important balding, middle-aged man with a small moustache and wearing a Fair Isle sleeveless pullover, glared at me. "I have lost my driving licence," I explained. He passed me a foolscap form with an ill-disguised expression of impatience, but without comment. I took the form over to the counter on the other side of the room, where there were two short, blunt pencils, each attached to the wooden frame with coarse string, just as if anyone in their right mind would want to steal them. The string was not quite as long as the form, and so I had to fold it to complete it, only spotting the instruction 'Do not fold this form' when I got to the end.

I returned to the hatch - closed once more - and tapped on the glass. "Yes?" 'I have completed the form, except for one section," I told him. "You have folded it!" he observed accusingly. "The strings on your pencils are too short," I remarked. "Nobody else has complained about that. Now, what is the section you haven't completed?" "5b," I replied. 5a required me to delete the alternatives which did not apply: *'My Driving Licence has been...Lost / Confiscated / Mutilated'*. 5b simply asked me to *'State Circumstances'*. "You have to complete 5b," he insisted. "I can't process the form unless 5b is filled in." I tried logic. "My licence is lost. If I knew the circumstances, I could find it, but I don't so I can't." He was resolute. "I can't process this form with 5b left blank. You'll have to write something in the box."

As so often happens at moments of apparent impasse, I experienced an inspiration. "Suppose you had lost *your* driving licence," I suggested to him. "What would you write in 5b?" He gave me a glassy stare. The tables had been turned upon him in a way that was clearly unexpected and unwelcome. "Advise me," I requested, enjoying his unproductive silence. Then, for the first time, he actually smiled. "I know!" he exclaimed, clearly enjoying a eureka moment. "Put *'mislaid'*." "Doesn't that mean the same as 'lost'?" I enquired. "Never mind..put *'mislaid'*."

ONWARD AND UPWARD

Of the new colleagues who later joined the teaching staff at John Rigby, two were of particular importance to me. The first was Kevin Sharkey, who came as Head of the Technical and Art Department, replacing Ozzie Waring, who moved to a post nearer his home in Haydock with the dubious pleasure of teaching girls with behaviour problems. The second newcomer was Brian Lewis, my friend and fellow art student, who joined the staff to work alongside me.

Kevin was my new boss. This was because Art was still part of the Technical Department at that time. He was a highly experienced teacher with a clear policy for his subject, and the woodwork lessons gained greatly in their effectiveness under his leadership, not least because he was a strong disciplinarian. Quite clearly, no more Evostik would be ordered for woodwork lessons whilst Kevin was in charge!

Brian Lewis had chosen to enter National Service after taking his National Diploma in Design, and had served with the RAF in Germany. After being demobbed, he worked in commercial art, but he had no strong career idea at that stage. Then, when the position of Art assistant became available at John Rigby, I persuaded Brian to apply and, simultaneously, sang his praises to Brother Ambrose. For the first half-term, Brian was appointed as a part-time teacher, with a timetable containing Art and Games, for two and a half days per week. By the end of October, Brother Ambrose had noted the quality of his new colleague's contribution, and had

41

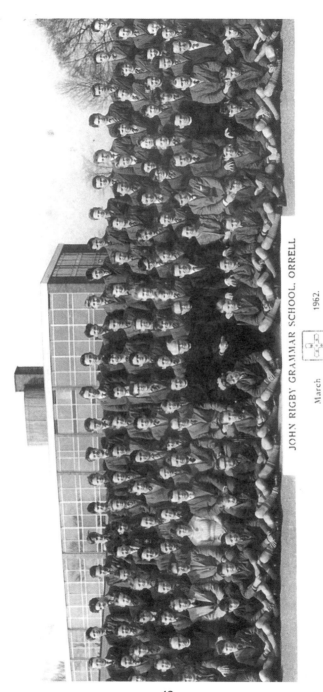

JOHN RIGBY GRAMMAR SCHOOL, ORRELL

March 1962.

The centre section of a full school photograph taken in Spring, 1962.
The author is on the teachers' row, seventh from the right

offered him full-time teaching. Brian happily accepted and, thereafter, gave up the idea of a career in graphic design, much to my satisfaction.

In the summer holidays, between Brian Lewis's appointment and the beginning of term, I spent some time introducing him to the art course and, in particular, to the History of Art syllabus. Because of the excellent weather, we held our meetings on Birkdale beach, and we must have appeared most eccentric to other sunbathers, surrounded as we were by piles of reference books. Still, it seemed to work, and Brian's arrival in the department enabled us to strengthen the quality of Art education at John Rigby, as well as giving me a colleague to discuss plans with.

Brian and I had looked forward to putting our plans into operation at the beginning of the new school year, although I have no doubt that he was somewhat apprehensive at starting in a profession that was new to him. Matters were not helped by the timetable not being ready by the first day or, to be strictly accurate, for the first two weeks. Staff were simply allocated to year groups and told to get on with things on an ad hoc basis. I found this intensely annoying and, inexcusably, it was to happen more than once. In the USA, President Kennedy was facing difficulties of a similar order - I had the frustration of an unfinished timetable; he had the problem of the Cuban Missile Crisis! I knew how he felt.

SHOCK OF THE NEW

By far the most serious event of 1962, and probably of the second half of the twentieth century, was the Cuba Blockade, instituted by President Kennedy in response to the covert building of Soviet missile sites on the island of Cuba. The President gambled on Krushchev backing down and dissembling the sites, which is what happened, but there is no doubt that the world was closer to an all-out nuclear war on that occasion than at any time since 1945. The Soviet leader lost credibility as a result, and was 'retired' from office in 1964 to make way for Brezhnev and Kosygin. The story is that, when Krushchev returned from holiday, his position had already been carved up by his colleagues, which only goes to show the danger of taking holidays if you are in power.

By halfway through that year, the Sixties really had begun to move at a faster pace than anything we had experienced previously. In the film industry there was David Lean's 'Lawrence of Arabia', 'The Birds' by Alfred Hitchcock, the very first James Bond movie - Dr No, and 'Lolita', which most people considered shocking. A different kind of shock came with the death of Marilyn Monroe, most probably the best known woman of her day. Rumours of suicide and a relationship with President Kennedy spread. In this country, Harold MacMillan sacked seven members of his cabinet, in what was described as 'The Night of the Long Knives', to liven up a Tory government in decline. Cartoonist Vicky christened him 'Mac the Knife', and Liberal MP Jeremy Thorpe observed: "Greater love has no man than this, that he lay down his friends for his life."

A less deferential approach of satire appeared in the form of the irreverent magazine, 'Private Eye', which first appeared in February of that year. In similar vein came the new TV programme, 'That Was The Week That Was', introduced by David Frost, directed by Ned Sherrin, and featuring Willie Rushton, Millicent Martin, Lance Percival, Ronnie Barker, Ronnie Corbett and other young emerging personalities. It appealed to all those who considered British society in general, and the television companies in particular, too stuffy and fawning.

An example of the sharp humour was exemplified by David Frost as he closed a show in October, 1963. Lord Home, who renounced his peerage to become Sir Alec Douglas-Home, was the incumbent Prime Minister who faced the Labour leader, Harold Wilson, in the following year's election. Frost observed: *"And so, there is choice for the electorate: on the one hand, Lord Home - on the other hand, Mr Harold Wilson. Dull Alec versus smart-alec."* The BBC received 310 letters and 599 phone calls of complaint. 'TW3', as it became known, was dropped in November 1963.

Another new television programme was the Police series 'Z Cars', which brought a new hard reality to the presentation of policing on TV, particularly when compared with the rather cosy 'Dixon of Dock Green' that people had become used to. The senior detectives of this new series were Stratford Johns as Inspector Barlow and Frank Windsor as Sergeant Watt. The setting was Newtown - clearly based on Kirkby near Liverpool - where I was subsequently to teach.

A most intriguing documentary appeared as part of Granada TV's 'World in Action' series at that time. It was entitled '7 Up', featuring interviews with, and shots of, a group of seven-year-olds from various parts of the country and from widely differing social classes. They were observed in school, at play and in conversation with their friends. At the end, all of them were brought together in a playground. Director Michael Apted's plan was to track children throughout their lives, at seven-year intervals, to see how far the Jesuitical belief: 'Give me a child until he is seven and I will show you the man,' holds water. '14 Up' followed in 1970, 21 Up in 1977, and the most recent programme, '35 Up' was screened in 1991. For those who complain today that there is simply nothing worth watching on TV, shown below is the available viewing in August 1961!

BBC. 1.00-1.30 pm Welsh News & Today, rpt 2.00 News 2.05-2.20 Picture Book (for the young) 5.00 Blue Peter 5.20 Crunch & Des 5.45 Seeing Stars - The Giant Planets 6.00 News 6.07 Regional News 6.17 Weather 6.20 Look - Seashore, rpt 6.50 Tonight 7.29 News 7.30 Overland

Trail 8.20 Africa Now -Ghana 9.05 'Jack's Horrible Luck' (play) Wilfrid Bramble, Barry Foster 10.00 News, Sport 10.15 Just for a while - Old time Dancing: Sidney Bowman Orchestra 10.45 Weather 10.48 Close down

ITA (Granada) 4.50 pm Dizzy Date 5.00 Seeing Sport: Lawn Tennis 5.25 Ivanhoe 5.55 News; Piano Pops 6.10 All Our Yesterdays 6.30 Robin Hood 7.00 Criss Cross Quiz 7.30 Coronation Street 8.00 Three Live Wires 8.30 Bonanza 9.25 News 9.35 Harpers W1 10.30 Another World - Sitting Tenants 11.00 News 11.10-12.05 'Once A Sinner' Part 1 (film) rpt.

In popular music, the Beach Boys were starting to build a growing reputation in the USA, but nothing very exciting was going on over here until November, when Brian Lewis, Tradge and I went to the Arts Ball at the Palace Hotel in Birkdale. In between the two live bands (one of which was the Merseysippi Jazzmen, who are still performing to this day at the Hesketh Arms in Churchtown Village on Wednesday evenings) a DJ was playing records. Tradge asked me if I had heard of this new group from Liverpool whose song was being played, and whom he had seen live at The Cavern Club in Mathew Street. I hadn't. The group was 'The Beatles' and the song was 'Love Me Do', which got to number 17 in the charts at the end of the year. I thought the song was pleasing, but nothing special. I didn't imagine that the group would amount to anything. Decca Records took much the same view: "We don't like their sound. Groups of guitars are on the way out." Decca and I - we knew a thing or two.

Most young people reach an age when they want to be different from their parents, and we were no exception. However, the degree of that difference in the 1960s was notably larger than before, and has continued to grow, generation on generation. Popular music was no longer something just to listen to or to dance to; it was very much an expression of a new, liberated age, and the sentiments expressed in the lyrics belonged to us, just as much as to those who wrote and sang them. To a great extent, this is why the playing of an old song graphically re-awakens memories of a love affair, a holiday, or some other life experience from our youth.

Shared experiences of the kind felt by those aged 16 to 30 at this time gave us all a sense of solidarity that, in many ways, transcended class, wealth and gender. Needless to say, it was naive and unknowing, but none the worse for that, particularly when contrasted with the sharp-eyed cynicism that has developed and flourished since, and which appears to have threatened the freedom for today's teenagers to be truly themselves. Periodically, they are required to defer to the benchmarks and references that deny their individuality by determining it.

But I am viewing life and values from another age, so perhaps I am mistaken. W H Auden warned us against evaluating the past in the light of what we have learned and absorbed since.

45

PLEASE PLEASE ME
1963-66

196319631963196319631963196319631963

LONDON EXPERIENCES

Although I had been on few school trips as a schoolboy at KGV, I was keen to organise educational visits as a teacher. John Mockett had enthused about a five-day London trip he had attended with West Derby High School, where he had undertaken teaching practice. Bob Mossman, the Head of the Art department, led a group of about 60 boys around all the major sights of the capital, and they stayed at King George VI Memorial Hostel - the YHA's flagship - in Holland Park, Kensington. I decided that this would be an exciting venture for me to undertake, and I approached my Head with plans for a 5-day residential visit in January, 1961. Quite rightly, he ruled out the idea of a teacher with only one term's experience leading what was quite a complex operation but, just twelve months later, I was at last able to persuade him of my ability to make the project work.

After the Art Society London Trip was announced, more boys than I expected asked to take part, and so I had to draw lots to make up the party with a few reserves, making a mental note to include those who were unlucky on next year's trip. An amazing example of naivety was shown by my failure to keep a list of what each boy had paid me as money began to pour in. I simply took their word for it when they told me they had paid in full and, although I'm quite sure that they were all completely honest, any memory lapses would most certainly have cost me dearly. I now find it hard to believe I was so green.

That pioneering 5-day London Trip from John Rigby left Wigan North Western Station early in the morning of January 2nd, 1962. Quite amazingly, the cost to each of the 30 boys was £4.10.0. That included return rail fare, all Underground fares, four nights bed and breakfast, evening meals at the youth hostel, entrance to anything where a charge was payable, and full travel insurance. The only expense for the boys, apart from presents, sweets and souvenirs, was the mid-day lunch, which I had booked in advance at a number of locations, including the Natural History Museum's caféteria and the Fish Bar on Tottenham Court Road. Pocket money was collected by agreement and given out to boys twice per day on request.

Because of the young age of the party, no-one was allowed out unaccompanied, and so the itinerary was organised for the evenings as well as during the day. We arrived back at Wigan in the evening of January 6th after an exhausting but highly enjoyable experience of the capital. As the platform emptied of group members and their parents, one boy thanked me and another said "Sir, me mam says I've to thank you". Not one parent spoke to me. This was my very first encounter with what proved to be commonplace behaviour by parents after residential trips, whether in the UK or abroad, and was not peculiar to this school.

The January London Trip became a fixture in the calendar of the John Rigby Grammar School, and I ran eight of these before leaving in 1969. The Warden of the hostel was Grace Markham, a figure very much like Margaret Rutherford, star of several British comedy films in the 1940s and 1950s. She and her slightly eccentric husband, Guy, eventually became good friends of mine. Guy had an oblique sense of humour, nowhere better exemplified than in the tannoy announcements he would make from time to time. He spoke in a slow, deep voice that would not have been out of place in a Hammer horror film: "Hostellers are reminded that the door of the hostel closes at 11.30, and that it is a long, cold night in Holland Park after midnight, with the frost attacking your very bones!" One of our boys, hearing this, added: "And no talking in the gas chambers!" I don't know what foreign hostellers made of Guy's messages, but I do remember well an occasion when he was severely reprimanded by YHA inspectors who failed to see anything amusing in his eerie monologues.

London was an exciting place to visit in the 1960s. Quite often we would take the party on a Thames boat trip from Westminster Pier on that

47

first night and, over the years, I became good friends with boatman, Stan Hawkes and his family. The view of the capital from the new Post Office Tower was spectacular, Hamley's Toy Shop was a schoolboy's delight, and Carnaby Street was quintessentially of its period, full of 'today's' youth fashions. One of the leading designers of the day was Mary Quant who opened Britain's first boutique. "Young people are tired of wearing essentially the same as their mothers," she proclaimed. I certainly agreed with that! I actually bought a cherry red brocade waistcoat from Lord John of Carnaby Street during one of the trips. Just as I was paying for this rather daring item, the assistant asked me if I would be interested in the entire suit - a long, flared jacket with matching hipster trousers in the same red brocade. "Perhaps sir would like to try it on," he suggested. Sir declined.

The average number of boys I took annually to London was about 45, but, in January 1965, I decided to increase the size of the party to 60. This required raising the number of staff to six, and one of these was the Head of Physics, Frank Miller. Frank's main hobby was photography, and so I asked him to take a group shot of the party on the steps of the hostel one morning before we left for our day's visits. The large crowd of boys gathered as requested at the main entrance. They were in good humour and looking forward to the day. Frank then started a long series of calculations related to focal length, appropriate exposure, the speed of film, and other apparently necessary procedures...ad nauseam. After ten minutes, the group had become so bored that the resultant photo, shown in this section, conveys the most dismal picture imaginable. Frank's cheery instruction to 'Say Cheese!' brought, from some boys, responses that I cannot record here.

At the end of the December term, every member of the party was provided with a detailed booklet showing the programme for the trip and including a map of the London Underground, and this was partly to show parents that they were getting good value for money. Although the organisation may appear prescriptive, I took the view that it is easier to change a pre-planned itinerary than to improvise on location.

As on all trips, there was a need for procedures to be laid down for when things go wrong, such as missing the Underground train, getting off at the wrong stop, becoming detached from the group, and so on. These were written into the printed programmes issued to all members of the party, and reinforced verbally. Whenever they were needed, which was not very often, they worked effectively. The major problems occurred, not when boys were lost, but when they did the opposite of what they were told.

The first example of disobedience took place at Crewe on the journey home. Everyone was instructed not to get off the train during this short stop. Despite this, Jimmy Matthews and Michael Mullaney decided

48

King George VI Youth Hostel in Holland Park, Kensington

A London Trip party 'subdued' by a delay (see p.48)

to visit the snack bar and, as the train whistled before departing, they ran onto the platform and jumped into the nearest carriage. As the train pulled out, our carriages set off for Wigan, but those occupied by James and Mick remained in the station. Crewe was where the London train split into two, and they had accidentally joined the section that was bound for Preston. I remained at Wigan North Western Station for a further hour and a half after the rest of the group had departed, in order to greet the two miscreants - after all, I still had responsibility for their care. I told them I would run them home, and they seemed grateful, if slightly puzzled, at my generosity. "You can drop me here, sir," said Matthews, as we got to the end of his road. "Oh no, James," I replied. "I'm coming in with you!"

The second time I was let down by senior boys was more serious. There were four Sixth Formers who, on the last night of the trip, went out for a drink. Although this was not permitted, I knew it was going to happen from time to time, and I would not enquire into any 17-year-old's behaviour as long as he did not shown the signs of having been drinking that might have been spotted by younger boys. These four had found a bar and decided to work their way along the top shelf - from Whisky to Brandy to Gin to Rum, and so on. They were so late back that the hostel doors had been bolted, and they had no choice but to climb over a wall that was five feet high on one side, but had an eight foot drop on the other, almost resulting in one of them breaking his leg. It was the noise they made when entering the dormitory block that inevitably led to their discovery. When I confronted them, two were white with fear, a third was weeping and apologising, and the fourth, most drunk of all, swore at me.

Throughout the next day, the last of the trip, these four boys made several attempts to talk to me and to apologise for their actions. I refused to speak to them until we were on the evening train home, partly to make them sweat, but also because I was too angry to be bothered with them. When we did discuss the issue, I told them how let down I felt. I decided that I would not visit the parents of the two boys who were the least drunk, partly because the father of one of them had died not so long before. As for the other two, I told them to go home from the station and to tell their parents that I would call in before going home to Southport.

Before heading for home, I made my two visits to the families as promised. There was an amazing contrast between their respective attitudes. At the first house, mother and father were so condemning of their son's behaviour that I found myself urging them to be lenient with him, mainly in view of his contrition and his previous good record. At the second, the response was rather casual, and both the mother and the father observed that "boys will be boys, won't they?" In this home, I struggled to persuade them that much was wrong with their son's attitude.

50

PUTTING ON THE STYLE

Clothes and matters of fashion were women's concerns. Well, weren't they? Men didn't really bother about what they wore. To be exact, they gave the impression of not bothering, particularly when talking to each other. After all, in 1963 it was still considered effeminate to wear after-shave lotion, and hair spray wasn't even thought of, unless you wanted to look like Dusty Springfield.

I wanted to be the sort of man who planned quite carefully the kind of clothes he wore, whilst giving the impression of complete indifference towards his appearance. In that respect, I was a typical male twenty-something of the early Sixties - smooth, nonchalant, urbane, casual. It was an unrelaxed way of appearing relaxed; a studied attempt to appear completely unstudied.

The two Southport shops that sold high fashion for men in those days were Orry's and Estorille, both on Lord Street and both well beyond my budget. Their clothes, particularly their sports jackets, were highly desirable, but jaw-droppingly expensive. I did manage to afford a pair of olive green leather shoes from Orry's in 1963, but their jackets were simply beyond my limited means. The fashions at Estorille were even further off the scale, and so all I could do was to press my nose against their window with an unfulfilled longing. I wasn't *that* bothered!

Then I had an inspiration. Burton's clothes were affordable but dull. Why not go to Burtons and see if they would make me a suit to my own design. Almost always, ideas such as this end in disappointment. *"Sorry, Mr Bagshaw, but we don't make suits to customers' designs."* This time, the dream came true, and the man at Burton's told me that he would be pleased to see my drawings and to make a suit to my requirements, just as long as I appreciated that the cost would be rather more than their off-the-peg range. I was happy with that.

I worked for several days on the cultivating of my new image. The suit would be in charcoal grey with a double mid-grey stripe in Italian style. Whilst the trousers were to have no turn-ups, the jacket sleeves would, and they would also have three fabric buttons on each sleeve. The jacket itself was to have four buttons, slim lapels and square ends - a double breasted finish on a single-breasted garment. The trousers would have eighteen inch bottoms, a size that reflected my consciousness of fashion without submitting to the gauche extremes of teenage overstatement. I was particularly keen to have a double-breasted waistcoat, but this would have increased the cost beyond my means, and so it had to be dropped. Most exotic of all was the vermilion lining, at extra charge, but what the hell! It took Burton's six weeks to make my suit, but the wait was worthwhile.

The finished product exceed my expectations and I felt distinctive and fashionable in my own design. I really didn't care what anyone else thought. Well, not that much. I got the maximum possible use out of that suit over the years, latterly wearing it well beyond its serviceable life. In the end it began to appear dated, and this represented a much greater problem than frayed trouser-bottoms.

As the sixties progressed, men's styles blossomed in a way that we could not have anticipated, making my one and only excursion into fashion design seem rather conservative by comparison. Still, it was fun while it lasted, and there is no doubt that I still miss that vermilion lining, if not the suit that it adorned.

THE MERSEY SOUND

I had been a devotee of classical music since I was first exposed to it as an infant by my father. Even the drama and force of Rock n' Roll had not attracted me to buy pop records, for I preferred to spend my money on Beethoven's Ninth Symphony or Bach's Schübler Chorales, although I listened to the Top Twenty from time to time. Despite 'Love Me Do', the Beatles first hit, being pleasant to listen to, it was not particularly ground-breaking. That was my feeling then, and it has not changed since.

'Please, Please Me' was altogether different. It was fresh and exhilarating in a way that I had not encountered before. The four-part harmonies added to the energy of the song and, like many other young people at the start of 1963, I listened to it over and over again. This *was* ground-breaking, but I do not think any of us had any idea how wide and sustained the influence of Beatles music was to be, and certainly Decca records hadn't rated them, having famously turned them down. In April, the group achieved their first number one with 'From Me To You', and this was followed by 'She Loves You' and 'I Want To Hold Your Hand' before the end of the year. Gerry and the Pacemakers enjoyed similar success, reaching the top of the charts with 'How Do You Do It', 'I Like It', and 'You'll Never Walk Alone'. There seemed then to be no end to the supply of Liverpool pop groups - The Searchers, The Merseybeats, The Fourmost, The Swinging Blue Jeans, Billy J Kramer & The Dakotas, Rory Storm & The Hurricanes - writing and performing songs that caught the imagination of the period. London was no longer music's capital.

Early in 1963, I wondered whether I should consider changing my Mini, but I was not sure of Mark's reaction to this. After all, is it right to sell a present without consulting the giver? My interest was aroused by the new Morris 1100, in many ways the Mini's elder brother. My letter to Mark Watson not only brought his agreement that the decision was sensible, but also an unexpected £250 cheque to assist with the exchange. Frank Balmer, my PE colleague at John Rigby, was interested in the same model, and so we eventually bought identical cars from Len Nuttall in Chorley.

I was delighted with everything about the new 1100 apart from the colour. Primrose yellow was somewhat disappointing when you have set your heart on British Racing Green, but the discount Len offered us applied only to these two vehicles. I decided to customise my new car and, with this in mind, I approached Charlie Dix, who ran a car repair and respray business at the bottom of Shakespeare Street in Southport. He sprayed the roof and wheels olive green, whilst my colleague from the School's Technical department, Roland Duckett, cut a dashboard of my own design from a piece of 'mahogany' formica. I painted white walls on the tyres to complete the transformation. Fantastic!

I associate the 1100 with two strange episodes. After Brian Lewis married Carol in 1964, they went to live at Burscough, and I used to pick him up on my way to school. One morning, Brian was waiting in the usual place when I approached but, oddly, did not stop to collect him. As I ascended Parbold Hill, I recall saying: "Oh, Brian, I wanted to ask you about...." I turned to look at him, but he wasn't there. In deep thought, I had forgotten to pick him up, and I had to return to Burscough at top speed to correct the mistake. "I knew you'd miss me eventually," he observed.

The second incident occurred on a sunny Friday afternoon. I had a large pile of Fourth Year examination papers to mark, and I put them on the roof of the car whilst I opened the driver's door. The inevitable then happened. As I drove down Gathurst Hill, I was aware of fluttering white objects in my rear-view mirror. It took me twenty minutes to find and collect all the sheets, for I could not afford to leave even one behind. I imagine some of the boys were rather puzzled when they received their papers back, a number bearing muddy smudges.

PRIDE BEFORE A FALL

The quality of much of the work produced by boys on art courses was improving in leaps and bounds, and the time that many of them must have spent on homework assignments reflected their enthusiasm, commitment and skill. I had not considered this would cause any controversy until, one day in the staff room, I received a complaint from a colleague that three boys had failed to finish his homework because their Art had taken them longer than expected. This comment prompted an even stronger complaint from another member of staff that his Third Year homeworks had been so rushed two days ago that he had told the entire form to repeat them. "They are wasting far too much time on Art!", he challenged. I was pleased at this, in a rather immature way, although I failed to pick up the strength of feeling in these comments at that time, perhaps believing they were only half serious. I was not to know that a few of my senior colleagues were airing their resentment over the popularity of Art and its effect upon their subjects, with the Head and his Deputy.

As the period for the school's first O level exams approached, I felt my anxiety rising, even though I had confidence in the boys' ability to perform well. On the days when the Art papers occurred, I experienced the attacks of nerves of the kind I had become so well accustomed to on the touchline during key Rugby matches, although much more accutely, because the outcome this time was of much greater importance. Waiting for mid-August was almost intolerable, and certainly much worse than when I, myself, had been sitting exams. What I was hoping for was not simply a reflection of my personal achievement as teacher; it was the wish for the boys themselves to attain what I felt they deserved by their magnificent efforts over the preceding three years.

Results day came, and I drove into Gathurst as calmly as I could, considering the tension gripping me. The grade sheets had arrived, but I was not yet able to see them because the Head and Deputy were studying them behind closed doors. Just as I felt able to cope with the waiting no longer, Brother Ambrose came out of his study and, with a proud smile, offered his congratulations on the quality of the Art results, and invited me in to see the printed Joint Matriculation Board lists. I was so thrilled. 32 out of 36 had passed and, expressing the exam results in today's grade equivalents, there were 8 at A*, 2 at Grade A and 6 Grade B. Maths and Art had gained the best results of all subjects on the timetable and, for some time to come, I walked on air.

The September that followed seemed to reflect the magic of the previous month's exam performance. Nothing at all could now go wrong, or so I believed. When I received the Art timetable for the year - on time on this occasion - I noticed to my concern that Form 5A, whom I had taught for the previous three years, did not appear. Clearly, a mistake had been made, and so I went to see the Head about it. There was no mistake, he informed me. There simply was not sufficient time in the week to fit in Art along with everything else. My belief that I had at last established my subject on a par with others was clearly premature, and rather reflective of the grammar school ethos of the period. This, then, was the extent of his explanation, although he did display some embarrassment in attempting to defend what I perceived, quite justifiably in my view, as indefensible. I strongly detected the inky fingerprints of other senior colleagues on this, although I had no way of being absolutely certain. My pleasure at the thought of boys spending more time on Art than on their other homeworks was wearing thin and had begun to lose its charm. Quite clearly, it was now payback time.

I left Brother Ambrose's study and walked over to 5A form room. I told them, with barely-concealed resentment, that Art was not to be available to them on this year's timetable but, if any boys wished to sit the O level examination, I would be prepared to teach them after school for one lesson per week. I did not wait for a response, because I was too upset, such was my feeling of injustice, most particularly after the splendid exam results of three weeks previously. Three days later, when I had come to the conclusion that no-one in 5A would take up my offer, and that I was much more troubled by the lack of Art on the timetable than they were, a boy called John Woods came to see me. He told me that he had been asked to bring me the message that, of the 28 boys in 5A, 26 wanted to commit themselves for a lesson per week after school for the rest of the academic year. Of those, 24 stayed with it - week after week and month after month - and, when the O level results were received in that summer, 22 of them had passed.

Just before the beginning of the next school year, a parent called John McDermott came into school to see me whilst I was busy making preparations in the Art department. I was initially unnerved, for his son was one of the two who had failed. Although young John McDermott wrote superb essays on the History of Art, his practical work was irredeemably weak, and it was touch and go whether or not he could possibly scrape a pass which, in the event, he did not manage. His father, who was the headteacher of St Patrick's Junior School in Wigan, and a well-known local character, had come in especially to thank me warmly for giving his son an invaluable appreciation and understanding of Art. "He has passed nine O levels; he doesn't need ten. What you have given him is worth much more than that!" Not only had this parent valued what his son had received from the art department; he had made the effort to come into the school to tell me. Of all the gratifying moments in my teaching career, I cannot recall any that exceeded this.

Still smarting from the timetable affair, I went to ask Brother Ambrose if he would make me Head of Art, rather than leaving me a member of a larger department. I imagine that he welcomed the chance to make up, to some extent, for my disappointment, and so he told me that he would recommend the idea to the governors, but I would have to understand that, during that academic year, there would not be an allowance he could offer me. I was pleased, and I assured him that money was not the main issue, for I simply wanted independence, and I was proud to have the title 'Head of Department' at the age of twenty-five. The governors granted my request. When the post became a remunerated one twelve months later, it provoked resentment from a most unexpected source; one that I would never have anticipated.

55

REMOTE CONTROL

This year, I was to be form master of 2C, some of whom had been in my form already as First Year boys. They were lively and amusing and, although they behaved well for me and for several other teachers, they could be a handful for the less experienced, principally because they were all absorbed with, and highly adept at, practical jokes. I can still see Peter Cornwell's furry caterpillar squirming across my desk on the end of a piece of cotton during morning registration. Other notable characters were Joe Wallace, a very large boy who later became a teacher himself in the London area, and the tall and eccentric Paul McCormick, known to his form-mates as 'Zoony'.

In order to make my form behave in the lessons of others, I devised a scheme that would be inconceivable in schools of today. I chose a Form Captain, Paul Dickie, and a Vice-Captain, Leslie Taylor. Their main job was to keep a record, in the Conduct book I provided, of any misbehaviour and of punishments given to members of the form in lessons. I would review this book the following morning, with reprimands and further punishments for those 'who had let me and 2C down', unless they were able to provide convincing explanations. It offended my pride to consider that my form were perceived as poorly behaved.

The rest of the form appeared to understand that Paul and Leslie were simply doing their job, and I was not then aware of any resentment. Needless to say, this would now come under the category of 'grassing'. No teacher today would dream of employing it, and no pupil would be prepared to undertake it. I had chosen Paul Dickie as the Form Captain simply because he looked mature and sensible, and so he proved to be. However, it was not until the first reports evening of that year that I heard from Paul's parents about his rather patchy behaviour during the previous year. They didn't know quite what I had done, but it certainly appeared to have worked and, for that, they were extremely grateful. I still receive Christmas cards from Paul and his family forty years later.

So strong was my determination to monitor and control the conduct of 2C that, after hearing graphic descriptions of their rowdiness in one of the Chemistry lessons, I warned them that they would all be strapped if it should occur again. Two weeks later, it did. So it was that, at the end of morning school, I lined up all twenty-nine of those boys, asking anyone who thought himself innocent of misbehaviour to speak up, and then delivered one stroke on each hand to each boy. Inevitably, those at the end of the line received only a token slap, such was my increasing fatigue. A few days later, Brother Ambrose, having read my strange entry in the Punishment Book, saw me to question the sense of punishing everyone in the form, not so much on ethical grounds, but "for the sake of your health, Mr Bagshaw."

Eight members of my Form 2C in 1963

Tony Hilton (left), director of the 1970 film of 'The Fall of Harald Hardrada', in which hand-to-hand combat (right) was a feature.

I was not the only teacher at John Rigby who believed that the quality of his form's behaviour was a reflection of his effectiveness. Michael McMahon, who came to us from St Peter's School, was subjected to much ribbing in the staff room when it was discovered that a member of his form had been arrested for stealing a car. "A fine example of a form master, you are!", quipped Kevin Sharkey, ever ready to score an amusing point over a colleague. "I like to think," replied Michael solemnly, "that, had it not been for my influence, he might have stolen a bus!"

All form masters and form mistresses taught Religious Instruction and, within that context, they were expected to deliver sex education when boys reached an appropriate age - in those days, at thirteen or fourteen. The best story about that was told to me by a former pupil and, later, a teaching colleague, Mike Unsworth. His form were taught by a Brother (whom I shall not name) who once said to them: "I know what you fellers get up to when you're on your own, and it's a sin!" "Is it a sin if we wear gloves, Brother?" asked Bernard Hedley, one of the form jokers. "Not as long as they're boxing gloves, Hedley!" was the reply.

After attending an English Schools Rugby Football Union coaching course at Padgate College, led by Eric Evans, I took charge of the School Under 13 team, in which several boys from Form 2C were members. Contact with young people in a variety of contexts - in this instance, Art, Religious Instruction and Rugby - can build strong and fruitful relationships. With 2C it was even stronger because, at my own request, I remained their form master until they sat O levels. Of course, if you do not get on well, this can be bad as well as good. In our case, I think it worked.

EVENTS

In 1963, the boxer who was to become Muhammad Ali was still called Cassius Clay, and his loud-mouthed boasting made every boxing match he fought into a sell-out. His first meeting with British Champion, Henry Cooper, attracted great interest. Everyone hoped that Cooper, and his powerful left hook could silence the 'Louisville Lip'. On the night in question, we were drinking in the Carstairs Club, run by Norman Ashurst just off Lord Street, and listening to the boxing match on the radio.

Just before the end of Round Four, Cooper felled Clay with a jolting left hook and, had the bell not sounded, the American would surely have been counted out. The interval lasted for much longer than it should have done, largely because Clay's glove had been torn, presumably by one of his seconds who was desperate to gain time for his man to recover. Almost inevitably, the fight ended in the following round, with Cooper unable to defend himself on account of severe bleeding. If the left hook was the British boxer's strength, cuts were his weakness. Had he not suffered from

58

this disadvantage, he might well have become world champion. As it was, Cassius Clay won the fight, and later, as Muhammad Ali, went on to become the finest world heavyweight champion ever seen.

There were several events which affected the transport system. In March, Dr Beeching, who had been appointed by the government to re-organise the country's railway system, proposed the closure of 2,128 stations and the redundancy of 67,700 railway staff. Although the reality was not quite as drastic as his proposals, it was certainly bad enough. On the roads, new continental-style signs were introduced. Meanwhile, an almost unbelievable item appeared in the newspapers: *Britain's worst learner driver, Margaret Hunter, has been fined for driving on after her instructor jumped out, shouting 'this is suicide!'*.

Pope John XXIII died in June. Most Catholics thought he had been appointed as a caretaker until a young successor could be found. In reality, he radically changed the papacy by his warmth and humanity and, with the Second Vatican Council, modernised Catholicism in a way that was both necessary and popular. For me, the use of the vernacular in the Mass was long overdue, not least to end, for many, the relative impenetrability of worship. In a number of churches, the laity had been made to feel passive witnesses to a private ceremony conducted in Latin by barely audible clergy with their backs to the congregation. A further Vatican resolution, which few will now recall, was the approval of the principle of a fixed date for Easter, currently being discussed in relation to the proposal to re-organise the school year.

In the United States, Martin Luther King stirred the consciences of many, whilst strengthening the resolve of his enemies, with his eloquent plea for the acceptance of black Americans as citizens fully deserving of equality. In the August of 1963, he addressed an audience of 250,000 people assembled at the Lincoln Memorial in Washington DC:
"I have a dream that one day this nation will rise up and live out the true meaning of its creed: 'We hold these truths to be self-evident; that all men are created equal'."

His courage moved all those who believed in freedom, and Berry Gordy, the leading light of Tamla Motown music, recorded the speech. And then, an event of staggering proportions, every bit as dramatic as the recent disaster at the World Trade Centre on September 11th, 2001 in New York. President Kennedy was shot in the head as he was driven in an open car through Dallas, Texas on November 22nd, 1963. They say that everyone who was an adult then, still remembers where they were when the news broke. I was at the ABC cinema - then called the Palace - in Lord Street, Southport, but I cannot remember the name of the film, even though I can recall an announcement through the loudspeakers telling us all of the assassination. Lance Morrow wrote in Time Magazine:

"The real 1960s began on November 22nd, 1963...it came to seem that Kennedy's murder opened some malign trap-door in American culture, and the wild bats flapped out."

TONY HILTON

In the September of 1963 a most unusual man joined our staff as a teacher of History. His name was Tony Hilton and, although he was only about twenty-two, he possessed many of the looks and mannerisms of someone older and more venerable. He was very tall, very thin, with a long face, and wore a rather old-fashioned three-piece suit. In the four pockets of his waistcoat were his grandfather's pocket watch, fob, rosary and snuffbox. What on earth would the boys make of this Dickensian figure, we wondered? How long was he likely to survive at John Rigby?

In fact, Tony proved most successful in the classroom, not least because he was a very good scholar and a very fine raconteur, and he very soon developed into one of the School's most effective teachers. His eccentric appearance and manner seemed to intrigue, rather than to put off, his pupils, and he became a popular member of the staff. His relationship with older boys was particularly good and, when he started a series of 'method acting' workshops after school, a good number of them came along to join in. I imagine that, at the outset, up to half of the volunteers thought it was something of a laugh, but it was not very long before they became absorbed in the activity.

The first fruit of these drama sessions was a quality performance of Marlowe's 'Doctor Faustus', chosen partly because it contained only one female rôle - Helen of Troy - which was played by a girl 'borrowed' from Wigan Convent. Flushed with this initial success, Tony went on to produce the Chester Miracle Plays with colleagues, Rita Smith and Pat Heenan, and Brother O'Halloran, who was in charge of the plainsong choir. He also brought re-enactment to the History lessons, on one occasion in a film of 'The Fall of Harald Hardrada'. About a hundred excited eleven-year-olds, holding home-made spears, assembled on a cliff beyond the field at the back of the school, near to Porter's Wood. After warning them sternly about the dangers of misbehaving whilst holding dangerous weapons, Tony took one step backward and fell of the cliff - a landmark in the annnals of method acting. Whilst hanging from the edge by his fingertips, he summoned the presence of mind to observe, "Now, you see what I mean!"

Like all younger members of staff, J A Hilton was timetabled for games lessons, although he could never have been described as a sporty type. He shared a Rugby group with Ken Draper, a member of the Maths department. Since Tony knew nothing of the laws of Rugby Union, he took

60

charge of the whistle, whilst Ken instructed him when to blow. The image of these two running together around the Rugby pitch, with Ken periodically shouting "Blow, Misterilton!" was one of the significant archetypal sporting visions of the 1960s.

A major challenge for a new teacher is that of controlling older boys, who will invariably feel more confident than he does. One day, a particular Fifth Form boy was attempting to undermine the History lesson, and it was clear that decisive action would be required, and so Tony sent to the office for the strap and punishment book, in line with school procedure. He ordered the boy to the front, instructed him to hold out his hand and, using his full height, brought the strap down onto its target with maximum strength. The boy smiled. "Oh...the *pain*," he observed.

It was important to learn from the unsuccessful strapping episode. Tony decided that he would, if necessary in future, borrow a strap from one of the Christian Brothers, should he need to use one. The assumption was that those they used were more robust, and this was probably correct. The day came when a boy's subversive behaviour required correction. Once more, Tony used the strap but, on this occasion, with stronger belief in its effectiveness. As he swung the strap onto its target, Tony followed through and, to his horror, caught his own thumb on the edge of the desk. This was pain beyond words; the pain that dare not scream its name. "Be assured," Tony told the boy, "that this has hurt me more than it has hurt you!"

19641964196419641964196419641964

SPRING FLOWERS

The momentum of the new 'Sixties Culture' continued. Radio Caroline became the first pirate radio station, beating the government's ban on independent broadcasting by transmitting of popular music from outside British waters. This defiance ultimately forced the BBC to bow to demand and to set up Radio 1. Those who wanted uninterrupted pop music on radio before this had no choice but to listen to Radio Luxembourg, with a signal that varied from the barely audible to the almost acceptable.

The Beatles released their film 'A Hard Day's Night', the title being taken from an impromptu remark from Ringo one morning before a recording session. This was the year that Beatlemania conquered America, although Alan Livingston, the head of Capitol Records had said, in advance of their arrival in the United States, "We don't think they'll do anything in this market." They soon had the top five singles in the American charts and, in the following year, 55,000 people saw them play live at Shea Stadium. In the midst of the Beatles' success, The Animals, a group from the North-East, had a hit with 'The House Of The Rising Sun'.

61

John Rigby's undefeated Rugby team (see p.63)

John Sharkey and Paula Velarde on a London Trip

An event in the USA, with comparable interest to that of the Beatles' tour, was the defeat of the boxer who had been considered by many as impregnable, Sonny Liston. He was beaten by the young upstart, Cassius Clay, who changed his name to Muhammad Ali immediately after the dramatic fight. Despite rumours of fixing, Ali repeated this victory and went on to become the most celebrated boxer in the world. We all wondered how far history might have been changed had Henry Cooper hit Clay with that left hook ten seconds earlier in last year's encounter.

A sporting landmark was also reached at John Rigby in this same year. The Under 15 Rugby Team's 4-year record read: Played 62, Won 62, Lost 0; Points For: 1420, Points Against: 112. By any standards, this was magnificent and, in addition, eight boys played for the Merseyside team and one, John Lydon, for England. This did not go down at all well with some of the established Christian Brothers' Schools in the area - St Edward's, Liverpool, St Mary's, Crosby and St Anselm's, Birkenhead. It was what Frank Balmer, who must take considerable personal credit for these achievements, once described as "The young chicken kicking the old hens around".

It was around this time that I started taking Paula Velarde, a fellow art student from the late fifties, to some of the John Rigby functions, including a performance of 'The Mikado' and a 5-day London Trip. Brother Ambrose, whose eye for an attractive woman was well developed, found Paula enchanting, and he constantly asked me how she was getting on and when she might next visit the School. In years to come, when he was Head of Scotus Academy in Edinburgh, and she worked as a young painter in Morningside in the same city, they became good friends.

THE ICE-MAN COMETH

The most ridiculous activity I indulged in during the early part of 1964 was ice skating. With my friends, Brian Lewis and Carol Kenny, I went to the rink at Freshfield, across the road from The Grapes Hotel. As a beginner, I spent the first quarter of an hour clinging to the side and doing my best not to fall over. As my fragile confidence grew, I launched myself away from the side for about fifteen seconds of wild adventure, before lunging back to the refuge of the wall. As time passed, I started to become marginally more competent and, after about half an hour, I managed to complete a wobbly circuit without actually losing my balance, not least because other skaters had the skill and foresight to get well out of the way as I approached.

The great mistake was that of believing that I was now ready to skate away from the rink wall with its nearby support. I embarked upon a mazy circuit, dodging other skaters as they accelerated past me. The major error was to leave the relative safety of the outside lane. In no time at all, I was swept inwards towards a vortex of experienced automatons. Then, the very worst thing that can possibly happen to a fledgling skater happened. Without the slightest warning, I went up onto the jagged edges located at the front curved sections of the skate blades. This unanticipated hazard forced me to enter a rapid and alarming 'tip-toe' action. Anyone who can remember the cartoon film that featured the cat, Sylvester, and the bird, Tweetie Pie, will know exactly what I mean. This speedy tip-toe motion was performed by Sylvester as he attempted, with a devilish smile on his face, to make a silent approach from behind on his feathered victim.

As I was finally sucked into the epicentre of the ice-rink, I reached out for something to cling to as my balletic ritual dance approached its feverish climax. I grabbed at a nearby pullover and, as I fell, the pullover was stretched by the weight of my descending body. The wearer of the garment, lovingly knitted by his wife, was the large figure of Roy Beckett, proprietor of Southport HiFi & Audio - the town's leading retailer in its field. He had been a pupil with me at Farnborough Road School, and later at KGV, but we had not met for about fifteen years until this sudden encounter. I stared up at Roy, noting that his pullover had lengthened by at least six inches as a result of my unprovoked 'attack'. "Hello, Roy," I said. "Hello, Paul," he replied.

WIGAN

It was whilst I was an art student in the 1950s that I began to find Southport rather unexciting and superficial. Liverpool, where I completed my final year, had a much stronger magnetism, not least because of the widespread artistic acitivity, and my own home town simply could not compete. The later attraction to Wigan was somewhat different, for it was related to the people rather than to the town. They were slow to accept you but, when they did, it was both genuine and permanent. Values such as honesty and loyalty were solid and consistent; there was a refreshing lack of affectation, and people meant what they said. There were occasions when the frankness of opinion was off-putting, but the consolation in this was that the views expressed were sincerely held. Overwhelmingly, families in Wigan were strong and supportive. They generally respected teachers, and would usually back them up in disputes with their sons. They were justifiably suspicious of waffle.

Architecturally, Wigan in the Sixties had little to offer, but it is amazing how a fondness for the population can breed an affection for their environment. I made a number of strong friendships in the town during my nine years at John Rigby, and I am pleased that some of these outlasted my working time in the area. One of these was the Sharkey family who lived in Hornby Street. Kevin taught with me, and he and his wife, Marie, were warm and close friends to me throughout their lives. I was pleased, too, to follow the progress of their three sons, John, Tim and Bill, each of whom succeeded in his own way. My other good friends were, and thankfully still are, the Warren family, whom I mention in 'The French Connection' later in this book.

Although it is now a tabloid newspaper, 'The Wigan Observer' of forty years ago was probably the widest paper in existence, and it was rumoured that Wiganers had longer arms than anyone else, simply as a result of reading it on a regular basis. Back in those days, Wigan Little Theatre had a strong influence, not least upon the three 'actor managers' of Wigan - John McDermott Senior, Dacre Brown and John Clayton. I was recently most disappointed to notice that this theatre has now become isolated by the new road system.

Wigan School of Art played a part in the education of those boys at John Rigby who followed the A level art course in the late 1960s. We thought it would benefit them to study there for one evening per week, giving them the influence of other teachers and introducing them to the art school atmosphere. The Art School was pleased to have them, and I am confident that they, too, benefited from the experience.

Most towns have special meeting places, sometimes with romantic connections. The rendez-vous I used most frequently in Wigan was the Gas Showrooms in Market Square, although I had better point out, lest I should appear to poke fun at the town, that this was chosen as the most convenient place to stop for coaches taking school rugby teams to away fixtures. My other regular meeting place was 'The Griffin' in Standishgate, where I would regularly drive over on Friday nights for a few drinks with Kevin Sharkey, Tony Hilton and John Clayton, and in later years, with John McDermott Junior, Mike Unsworth, Brian Farrimond, George Herterich, Hugh Crooke and Laurence Wilson. Those Friday evening visits to 'The Griffin' in the later part of 1971 were life-savers for me, as my third autobiographical volume will explain.

SOUTHPORT

As the years went by I found that I was spending more of my social time in the Wigan area than in Southport. This was driven by a number of changes. Firstly, many of the friends I had made during my student days had moved on to work in other parts of the country. Secondly, life teaches you that, although you may have much in common with particular people in one context, this relationship does not necessarily survive a change of circumstances. Thirdly, I was building up a growing number of new friends in and around my place of work.

In the early part of the decade, several of us - Brian Lewis, Colin Graham, John Wood, Brian Geldard, Godfrey Hand, plus the frail, pale figure of Harold Porter - continued to meet in Southport, but always in a club rather than a pub. Our most frequented venue was the Carstairs Club, formerly Norman Gregory's, which had then been taken over from Bruce Carstairs by Norman Ashurst. On many evenings we would gather round the elderly piano and sing raucous songs until the effects of Flowers Keg, an appetising Stratford beer introduced by Norman, took its toll. Some of us still went to the occasional party at Tommy Shorrock's in Trafalgar Road, Birkdale, but time was moving on and, believe it or not, we were becoming more moderate in our life-styles. Perhaps we were at last growing up.

Southport was changing. Although that may appear an obvious point to make, it should be noted that, up to the 1960s, change was less common than today, and that change in Southport itself was both unusual and unpopular. In that respect, not much has changed in the intervening forty years, as letters of complaint to the local papers today will show. I am able to record some of these Southport developments, mainly with the help of supporting information kindly provided to me by local historian, Geoff Wright Jnr, to whom I am greatly indebted.

The late 1950s saw the start of a decline in cinema provision in the town. Between 1957 and 1959, the Plaza in Ainsdale closed and became the Moulin Rouge, then Tiffany's, then the Natterjack and now the Toby Jug. The Forum Cinema on Lord Street was demolished, leaving a building site that lay vacant for over thirty years before becoming Forum Court flats, and the Coliseum in Nevill Street closed and was turned into an amusement arcade. The impressive Garrick Theatre, which had become the Essoldo Cinema in 1957, lost even more of the dignity that its Art Deco style deserved by becoming a bingo hall in 1963. In the same year, the Congregational Church on the corner of Chapel Street was demolished, the site having been occupied since by a number of retailers, one of the longest-running being the stationers, Lonsdale Universal. The area occupied by the church schools became part of Littlewoods store. Churchyard graves were moved to Duke Street Cemetery.

The Trocadero, near to the Monument, closed in 1960 and is now half of the large Woolworth's store that connects Chapel Street with Lord Street. Even my own local cinema, the Bedford, had been turned into a service garage by 1959. The Scala Theatre, which had changed its status from a theatre to a cinema and back again, closed in 1962 and is now the car park of B & M Bargains on Kingsway. Just four years later, the Grand was re-built as a casino, and the sad demise of Southport's cinemas was almost complete, no doubt hastened by the popularity of television. I do not know when the Queens and the Regent cinemas eventually disappeared from the

The Palladium Cinema (centre), now Sainsbury, on Lord Street, Southport

The Palace Hotel with the Fishermens Rest pub on the extreme left

north of the town, but it is revealing to note that, from boasting thirteen cinemas in the 1950s, Southport in 1967 had only three - the Odeon, now J Sainsbury Ltd, the Regal, now retirement flats, and the Palace, presently surviving as the ABC.

As the decade moved towards its end, the 220-room Palace Hotel on the Birkdale seafront was demolished, leaving only the Fishermens Rest Pub as evidence of its existence. There had been a rumour that the hotel was haunted by the architect's spirit who, having discovered that his building had been erected back to front, committed suicide by jumping down a lift shaft to his death, You might think it odd that he noticed this 'error' only on the completion of the project and, if you think it all quite unbelievable, you would be correct. Not long after the disappearance of this Hotel, the Bandstand, part of the municipal gardens in front of the Cambridge Hall, was pulled down and a brutal concrete fountain took its place. A number of 'thinking' young people of the time took delight in pouring coloured dye or washing powder into this offensive object, and that was about as revolutionary as we....er...they got in those days.

In 1971, the YMCA building in Eastbank Street was demolished. Although I had not been a member, I was saddened by its disappearance because it was the location of my only sporting 'success'. Although I was an incurable football fanatic and, since starting teaching, busy learning to love Rugby once more, the only sport at which I could claim some talent at that time was table-tennis. At the YMCA in the early 1960s, I had taken a set from the then Southport Champion. He complained that I was using a sponge bat of the type that had recently been banned for tournaments. "They are still allowed in *friendly* games," I observed. He didn't smile.

1971 also witnessed the building of the new Chapel Street Station complex and the demolition of the Railway Hotel. Lord Street Station, operated by the Cheshire Lines Railway Company, had already changed its status in 1952, when it was refurbished as the Ribble Bus Terminus. Marks & Spencer moved from the other side of Chapel Street to occupy the new premises, their former ones being taken by Boots Chemists, and these were the prinicpal modifications to Southport town centre over the decade. Although many Southport residents were unsettled by the changes, it is worth observing that change, in itself, is neither good nor bad. However, over time it is inevitable, and those who cannot accept it are going to experience permanent discontent. Perhaps their time would be better spent, not on opposing change, but rather on influencing it.

AUTUMN GOLD

At the end of the summer term, Brother Ambrose left John Rigby to become the Head of Scotus Academy, Edinburgh. His successor was Brother

O'Halloran, formerly Headmaster of St Anselm's College, Birkenhead. They were quite different in personality and, initially, I found my new boss rather cold and informal. I later concluded that his rather distant manner was more a product of shyness than of aloofness and, as time passed, we began to get on rather well, even though our educational philosophies differed widely. He was prepared and, I suspect, happy to debate ideas with me and, if he found my approach somewhat arrogant for a teacher who was relatively inexperienced, he did not show it.

One lunchtime, Brother O'Halloran asked to see me in his study. He was aware that I had been given the title of head of department, but understood that this had not so far been recognised financially. He was now in a position to do so, and I was delighted at the prospect of receiving a Grade A allowance. The surprise came when the post offered was at Grade B, for this was unusual for someone of my age and experience. The only condition, he explained, was that I should not make this known widely to colleagues at that time. I agreed happily, and left the Head's room justifiably elated.

Two days later I was asked, once again, to call at the Head's room. On this occasion, he asked me why I had not honoured the condition to keep the news of my promotion largely to myself. I was unnerved and told him that I had felt there would be no harm in telling my close colleague, Brian Lewis, of my good news. He agreed, but asked if I had told anyone else. "Only Kevin Sharkey, but he is my friend," I said. "He would not object, I am sure." "Mr Bagshaw, I am afraid that you under-estimate human nature," replied Brother O'Halloran. I found this most upsetting and, for some months, my relationship with Kevin was certainly more distant than it had been. In retrospect, I can well understand that a mature man with a family, could well feel discontented at the promotion of a young colleague onto the same level as his own. Fortunately, our close friendship - one that I valued highly - was later restored.

Confidence in the Art department was riding high, but both Brian and I were ready for improvement, and we wanted to push forward with innovation and course development. With this in mind, I made contact with Kurt Rowland, one of the leading lights at Hornsey College of Art, where exciting developments in the field of Integrated Design were taking place. Kurt had recently published a set of design textbooks, which were both pioneering and attractive. Brian and I visited his department and discussed ideas with him that we hoped to implement at John Rigby. He was impressed by our plans, and we returned to school with a mission to persuade our colleagues in the Technical department to join us in the project. They did, but not quite with the same level of enthusiasm as our own, for I rather think they suspected me of 'empire building' at that time.

69

The author (left) as Best Man at the Wedding of Brian Lewis (right)

Despite this, our new course for Third Year boys, with the element of 'consumer product analysis', where groups undertook practical testing of such items as school chairs or writing implements, and then developed questionnaires to discover the opinions of their classmates, proved to be absorbing and popular. This was partly because they did not have to be 'good at art' to involve themselves successfully in the activities, but much learning took place nevertheless.

In August of that year Brian Lewis, my good friend and colleague, married Carol Kenny at St Paul's Church in Southport, and I was pleased when asked to be Best Man. I also chose Bach's Chorale 'Nun komm' der Heiden Heiland' for the service. Not long after that the Labour Party won a narrow majority at the October election, and took office for the first time in thirteen years under Prime Minister, Harold Wilson. We began to know the new faces of this new government - James Callaghan, Denis Healey, Barbara Castle and Richard Crossman. When, a good time later, Crossman's diaries were published, they described the convoluted speaking of the civil service, and proved inspirational to the writers of the television comedy series 'Yes Minister' as they developed the character of Sir Humphrey Appleby. This, along with 'Inspector Morse', became one of my two favourite TV programmes.

1965196519651965196519651965196519651965

LONG LIVE PICASSO

I felt strongly, and still do, that young people should be exposed to the culture of their own time: the music, the writing, the drama, the visual arts, and so on. Nearly all art was modern in its day, yet many retreat to the relative safety of past styles and accepted conventions as far as The Arts are concerned, and are quick to reject anything that crosses the bounds of their expectations. If anyone should be able to display an open mind, it should be a young person and, with this raison-d'être, I devised a course in aesthetics for fourteen-year-olds. It was my hope that, when these boys were in their forties, although they may no longer wish to paint, draw or produce sculpture, it was conceivable that they may want to look at works of art with some background information and experience. Of course, I did realise that my views were tinged with idealism, but I have been gratified to learn in recent years, from a number of Wigan men, the extent to which visual art remains important to them.

All boys had undergone a basic design course in their first year at John Rigby, undertaking practical exercises in the various formal elements such as colour, tone, light, texture, line and composition. This enabled them to recognise more in a picture than simply its subject matter. The aim

71

was to ensure that, three years later, boys could apply these acquired principles within the attempt to understand why the majority of people cannot seem to get anything out of most examples of modern art.

The reasoning put to the boys went as follows: Most people judge paintings by their subject matter and, most particularly, how 'real' objects appear to be. Common responses might be "This is a good painting because it features horses and I like horses," or "That tree looks so real you could almost touch it." If you judge a work on its closeness to reality, what do you do when the painting doesn't depict something real or, as in the case of abstract art, does not represent anything recognisable at all? You have a choice. You either admit that the work is beyond you, you attempt to unravel the mystery within it, or you dismiss it as rubbish. Most people choose the latter, preferring to identify ignorance in the artist than in themselves. These judgements are frequently made in a time span of about five seconds, simply because the effort of looking for hidden qualities and trying to understand them is greater than many are prepared to make. Strangely, most people readily accept music, which is overwhelmingly abstract, yet demand recognisable content in visual art. They want to know what a painting 'means', yet do not think to ask the same question of a piece of music.

Those in the fourth Year at John Rigby were therefore encouraged to look at Form - the 'how' - as well as at Content - the 'what', and this was achieved largely by asking them questions - just as Socrates did - rather than by giving them answers. The questions might be "Why do you think the artist has used a predominance of blue in the background of the picture?" or "What do you suppose is the reason for the artist painting all of the shapes in primary coloured dots?" This searching for answers, allied to the fact that their practical work consisted of producing pictures of their own design in the style of the twentieth century movements - Expressionism, Fauvism, Cubism, Surrealism, and so on - taught these boys the value of patience in the attempt to understand, and tolerance in the face of ambiguity. To me, these are valuable and permanent life skills and, for those mature enough to apply them, are quite often transferable to other contexts and situations.

The work of art that is more rich in mysteries and symbols than most is the huge mural, 'Guernica', painted by Picasso in 1937 to mark the horror of the bombing of the Basque capital during the Spanish Civil War. The attempt to analyse this picture by the asking of questions usually filled an entire 75-minute lesson, yet I can rarely recall any boy being either bored or completely baffled by it. One even made a copy of it on his bedroom wall, such was the effect it had upon his imagination. Another, 13-year-old John Sharkey, when describing in his written homework why

72

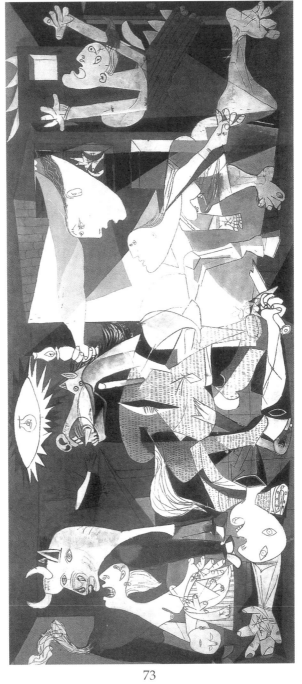

The huge mural 'Guernica' painted by Pablo Picasso in 1937

the mural had been painted in monochrome, wrote "suffering, stark and terrible, needs no colour to enhance it!" Everyone in these lessons was asked at least one question and, as the lesson progressed, the different symbols and their probable meanings were revealed: the horse, the bull, the light bulb, the dead soldier, the mother holding a dead baby, the refugee and the tiny flower. I had a most gratifying phone conversation just a few weeks ago with a former John Rigby boy, now 56 years old, who told me of his excitement at seeing 'Guernica' at first hand in the Museo Reina Sofia during a recent business visit to Madrid. "It made my trip. It was magnificent!" he told me enthusiastically.

When the time to sit O level arrived, the boys at John Rigby were entered for two practical papers, and one in the History and Appreciation of Art. A question that tended to appear quite frequently on the written paper was 'Write accounts of two works by a living artist, explaining why you have chosen them.' Since they all knew more works by Picasso than by any other artist still alive, this question was one they could look forward to with some confidence, just as long as the Spaniard survived until the day of that paper came round. In the mid-1960s, Picasso was over eighty years old, and many, including myself, prayed that, were he to be taken from us, it would be later rather than sooner!

FUN AND GAMES

Early in 1965, having just completed my fourth 5-day London visit with John Rigby pupils, I decided to look at the possibility of running an outdoor pursuits trip during the summer holidays. A survey suggested that this would prove popular, and so I decided to make an initial booking with the Holiday Fellowship for two weeks in August at their Newlands hostel. This was quite near to Hawse End Ferry at the eastern edge of Derwentwater on the other side of the lake from Keswick. I persuaded two of my colleagues, Kevin Sharkey and Brian Mullaney, a young Chemistry teacher, to join me, and the three of us set off from the Market Square in Wigan by coach with 40 boys in the party.

Unlike comparable trips today, the coach did not stay with us, for this would have been too expensive. This meant that, apart from using the ferry on odd occasions, we walked simply everywhere, yet I have no recollection of anyone complaining, even when we walked into Keswick for Mass on Sunday. We climbed Cat Bells and Causey Pike, neither being too difficult for fit young lads, and it was agreed that we would tackle Skiddaw, mainly for the breathtaking view it would offer. We set off with enthusiasm to scale England's third highest peak, although our sense of adventure was somewhat subdued by the sight of young women with small children passing us as they descended. We carried a rucksack with 43

74

Lake District Trip group at Newlands near Derwentwater in 1965
with teachers Brian Mullaney, Kevin Sharkey and the author.
The late Alan Cullen is on the left of the back row (see p.97)

Relaxing after erecting the tents at the 1967 camp

cans of Coca-Cola, and shared the carrying between us during the two and a half hours it took us to get to the summit.

Conquering Skiddaw proved a complete anti-climax for the entire party. Firstly, we found that the summit was shrouded in heavy mist, obliterating completely the view we had anticipated and, secondly, we had forgotten to pack a can-opener. This was just before the days of ring-pull cans, and you have my word that it is impossible to open a can by smashing it onto a rock. Descending, which took just over an hour, placed much greater strain on the legs than climbing, and it was an exhausted party that returned to the hostel that evening, thirsty into the bargain.

About a week before we set out on the trip, I had designed an initiative test with the help of a large scale Ordnance Survey map. Two days before the party left Wigan, Kevin Sharkey and I drove to Newlands and laid the various clues. One morning, in the second week of our stay, I announced to the boys that we would now do the test, and they were split into four groups. Off they went with joyful enthusiasm as Kevin, Brian and I took the opportunity to relax in peace for what we confidently expected to be at least three hours.

The groups had left the hostel at 10 am, armed with maps and cryptic clues, and we settled down for a restful morning in an attempt to catch up on lost sleep. To our horror, we heard the voices of the first returners at 10.50 and, by 11 am, all forty boys had returned. So much for our planned rest. The test that had taken me twelve hours at home to prepare, and two of us over three hours to lay, yet they had cracked it completely in under an hour! In almost every respect the trip was a success and, for some of the boys, it was probably their only summer holiday. Two years later we returned to Newlands, but in 1966, we ran a similar trip to Llandogo, not far from Tintern Abbey between Monmouth and Chepstow in the Cotswolds. I remember it well, mainly because we shared the hostel with a party from London who insisted on singing "We orl liv innar Yallow Sabmareeen" at every available opportunity.

In September 1965, the Merseyside Rugby Union under 15 group held a meeting at West Park Rugby Club in St Helens to plan for the forthcoming season. Usually, Frank Balmer, as head of Rugby, would attend but, on this occasion, he asked me to go. I suspect that I was set up - in the nicest possible way - for I was proposed as a committee member and duly elected. The proposer was Peter Gaskell, Deputy Head at Ruffwood School in Kirkby, and I later guessed that Frank had spoken to him in advance about my suitability. The truth was that, although I was immensely keen, I had neither the coaching experience nor the playing background to compare with most of the others. Nevertheless, it was the beginning of ten most enjoyable years as Merseyside selector, during which

I met and worked with some excellent colleagues, including Maurice Wright, Mike McLoughlin and Les Hooker.

Each year, two of our committee would serve on the Lancashire selectors' panel, and my turn came round in 1967. In the following year I was a selector for the North of England at the area trial held at Gosforth, and I must admit to feeling somewhat out of my depth when I looked round the room at the distinguished company. Despite this, my opinions were invited and listened to with respect, such was the courtesy of the senior members of the panel. My main disappointment was the failure of a John Rigby player, Gerry Prior, to make the North of England first team. Gerry was an inspirational scrum half who would often try the unexpected. In most cases, it came off, but there were times when it didn't. He was against a Cumbrian opponent who did everything by the book, giving the ball out every time and never taking risks. The fact that he was preferred outlined the difference in attitude that then existed between Welsh and English selectors. The English would pick the boy who made the least mistakes; the Welsh would go for the player with flair. On that basis, George Best, Gazza and Ryan Giggs would be passed over for safer soccer players, and that was Gerry Prior's fate on that afternoon on Tyneside. As a teacher at his school, it would have been considered unethical for me to have spoken up for him.

The highlight of alternate seasons was the Welsh Tour when we took about twenty-five Merseyside boys to the principality to play three games, usually against Gwent, South Glamorgan and Mid-Glamorgan. The boys were hosted by Welsh players' families, whilst we stayed in a hotel. The games were hard-fought, and a win here was always well earned. There was a tour when Merseyside remained undefeated, but it was some time after I had left John Rigby. At the end of each season we held our colour awards ceremony for boys who had represented the area, and former internationals Bill Beaumont and Mike Slemen were generous with their support and ever willing to present ties and certificates. The camaraderie was strong, and it was a maturing experience for boys from different schools and backgrounds to come together and to learn to play as a team. Many went on to gain county and national honours, but none was more talented and successful than a Wigan boy called Shaun Edwards who captained England Schoolboys at both Rugby Union and Rugby League, and enjoyed a most distinguished professional career.

SUCCESSES AND FAILURES

One of the weaknesses of the average grammar school was that it tended to concentrate its greatest efforts upon those in the highest ability range. This was evident at John Rigby from the middle of the decade, and

77

showed itself in two ways: the dismissive attitude of some of the teaching staff to boys in the D stream, and the substantial belief in the value of expressing.

The school had taken an extra form of entry - four rather than three - in the September of 1962. By the end of that academic year the one hundred and twenty boys had been placed in one of four streams: A, B, C and D. It was not long before comments were passed in the staff room about the advisability of recruiting an extra thirty boys, even though they had scores of 113 or more at the Eleven Plus examinations. Remarks along the lines of *"they shouldn't be here"* or *"they can't cope"* or, worst of all, *"I give up"*, incensed me and bred what was to become a growing unease with selection at eleven, and an increasing belief in the true value of the comprehensive system.

Earlier in the year, Labour's Anthony Crosland had posted a warning sign by promising "If it's the last thing I do, I'm going to destroy every fucking grammar school in England and Wales. And Northern Ireland." This was a stupid and iconoclastic polemic, mainly because destruction has no place in positive action, yet I sympathised with the principle of removing selection at eleven for the nation's children. So, when circular 10/65 appeared, requesting all the local authorities in the country to submit plans for comprehensive reorganisation, it seemed to me that a window had been opened on the dark recesses of a system that required failure in order to highlight success.

When plans were laid for the introduction of the new Certificate of Secondary Education, which provided an examination target for those of moderate ability, Brother Lennon, Head of Maths, declared that he was "lowering his standards for nobody!" As far as I was concerned, this attitude, held by many teachers in many grammar schools, completely missed the point of the exercise, which was to provide a tangible record of achievement for those who would otherwise have left school at the age of fifteen completely unqualified. Whether it would be applicable to the average grammar school child was irrelevant, but then the majority of grammar school teachers had little interest in the welfare of those from the other side of selection.

Headmaster Brother O'Halloran was an advocate of the express system, within which boys of high ability would take O levels after four, rather than five years and thereby gain an extra year in the sixth form, principally to facilitate Oxbridge entrance. To discuss this policy, he called a meeting of Heads of Department one lunchtime. In the ten minutes before the meeting, we argued the relative merits and demerits of this idea in the staff room, and the consensus was generally that there would be more to lose than to gain by its implementation. It became quite clear that most of my colleagues had serious reservations about the proposal. My own view was conditioned by experience, for I had been expressed at King George V School, and I did not feel that, on balance, I had gained from it. I was quite certain that I had lost a year of childhood in the process, and this was also true of my girlfriend's brother, Edmond Velarde, who was in an express stream at St Mary's College, the Christian Brothers School in Crosby.

In the meeting that followed, Brother O'Halloran explained his belief in the value of the policy and then went round the room asking colleagues in turn if they approved. With the exception of Harry Finch, Head of Geography, and myself they all capitulated, nodding sagely in response to their Headmaster's arguments and applauding the advantages of expressing for boys at John Rigby. Quite understandably, Brother O'Halloran drew the conclusion that, with two exceptions, his middle managers were solidly behind the idea and so it was adopted. As we trooped back into the staff room I completely lost my temper and shouted at my fellow teachers in genuine anger. My indignation was not as a result of losing the argument. It was simply a deeply-felt response to what I perceived as collegial hypocrisy.

1965 brought with it a number of interesting developments which might justifiably be described as successes. Edward Heath replaced Sir Alec Douglas Home as leader of the Conservative Party, the first of his kind to be educated in a state school - a grammar school - and the first leader to be elected, rather than appointed. By coincidence, this year marked the 750th anniversary of the signing of Magna Carta. Also, the death penalty was suspended, surely a reflection of a just and humane society. In England and Wales, 90% of the population had a televsion set and the viewing figures passed the 25 million mark.

At the beginning of the year, Winston Spencer Churchill died - a man who had spent six decades in parliament - and his funeral was an enormous state occasion, grander even than that of the Queen Mother in 2002, and justifiably so. Rhodesia made a Unilateral Declaration of Independence and matters became worse in Vietnam as the US Air Force started bombing raids. On a lighter note, the Beatles received the MBE, Philips launched the audio cassette and Manchester United were the champions of Division 1. Stanley Matthews, retiring at the age of fifty, was the first footballer to be knighted, Mary Whitehouse set up 'The Viewers' and Listeners' Association' and the millionth Mini came off the assembly line. You could buy a pint of bitter for 1/5d (7p), a bottle of whisky for 7/- (35p) and take a two-week break in the Costa del Sol for the sum of £66. We had 'Help' from the Beatles, 'Satisfaction' from the Rolling Stones, whilst the Moody Blues released 'Go Now' and Tom Jones sang 'It's Not Unusual'.

BOY RACER

Although I had enjoyed my customised Morris 1100, despite a failing gearbox after eleven months - fortunately repaired under guarantee - and both sub-frame mountings later going wrong, I now had my eyes on a Ford Cortina GT or, more precisely, a new, white Cortina GT with black vinyl upholstery and dashboard, four small round gauges for oil, water, fuel and temperature, in addition to the speedometer and rev counter, and a leather covered steering wheel. It stood in the showroom of Bradshaw's in Preston. It was gleaming and magnificent, and it was described as capable of accelerating from 0 to 60 mph in just nine seconds - impressive for 1966.

Mr Entwistle, the salesman, offered me a reasonable trade-in price for the Morris, and so I signed an order for the Cortina and paid a deposit, despite having little idea whether or not I could really afford it. The plan was to pay the balance over the next two years and, for someone with an appetite for instant gratification, the seduction of ownership totally obscured any other considerations. I added further to the cost by specifying a car radio - an optional extra in those days - and Pirelli Cinturato radial tyres, an absolute must for upwardly-mobile young professionals and boy racers like me!

The School London Trip, by way of a change, had taken place at the end of December, and so I travelled to Preston on Saturday, January 1st 1966 to collect the new car - CRN 170D. As I drove the Cortina GT out onto Marsh Lane, anyone watching would have thought that the vehicle was laden with shock-sensitive explosives, so careful was my driving technique and so graceful my speed. By the time I passed Lancashire Police Headquarters at Hutton, my initial caution had disappeared, and I exploited the GT's powers of acceleration to the full. It was not until I got as far as Mere Brow that I spotted a problem: the four gauges in the centre of the dashboard were all inactive. I hardly had time to get angry about this defect when another one struck - I ran out of petrol! Not only had I been given a car without a full pre-delivery inspection; I had been allowed to drive away from the showroom with less than half a gallon of petrol in the tank. What a way to treat a discerning motorist, I thought.

It took two further visits to Preston before the gauges were fixed, and I wrote down a list of complaints:

FORD CORTINA GT - CRN170D
Not working on delivery:
Oil Gauge, Fuel Gauge, Temperature Gauge, Passenger Air-Vent.
Not fitted on delivery:
Cigarette lighter, wheel trims, dust-caps on two tyres.

Further faults:
Serious exhaust trouble, Windscreen-washer fault,
Suspension trouble, Driver's door friction,
500-mile service booked, but not recorded or carried out.

I now assumed that no further hazards lay ahead. For about eighteen months, they didn't, but as my mileage passed the figure of 22,000, the first of a series of punctures to my prestigious Pirelli Cinturato tyres occurred. There was a period in the Autumn of 1967 when I suffered eight flat tyres in seven weeks. Despite all these frustrations, I enjoyed the driving of the Cortina GT on a much higher level than any previous car. The leather steering wheel, the black upholstery, the range of instruments, the innovatory air-vents, the acceleration, the body-hugging front seats and the centre armrest, not to mention the prestigious GT badge, all gave a gratifying sensation of well-being.

I was not the only one enjoying life in 1966. The Labour Party won the General Election with a 97-seat majority and, for the first time, I voted for them, principally because they were the first government to spend more on education than on defence and, generally, because they seemed to me to represent a greater fairness and compassion in their social policy, a view I still hold. Mao Tse-tung proclaimed the Cultural Revolution in China and, in Barcelona, police beat up 100 priests who were protesting against police brutality. History was made when the Archbishop of Canterbury visited the Pope in Rome, the first official meeting of its kind for 400 years. More significant to many of us were England winning the World Cup and the increasing popularity of the mini-skirt. It is hard to decide which of these gave greater pleasure to the English male. The 70 mph limit was imposed on motorists, Barclays launched Britain's first credit card, and oil and gas were discovered in the North Sea. The world's first vertical take-off and landing aircraft, the Harrier, was on show at Farnborough. Not everything was going all that well, however, particularly for the Beatles whose LPs were being destroyed by thousands of American teenagers after John Lennon told them that the group was 'more popular than Jesus'.

Although John Lennon's comment was far less extravagant than everyone believed, it did betray a measure of complacency quite common amongst aspirational young men in their mid-twenties. Like many others who have overcome their initial uncertainties in new roles, I was beginning to develop an inflated sense of my ability to achieve almost anything I wished in the teaching profession, and I think my friend, John Mockett, thought similarly at this stage of his career. I beheld just what I had achieved thus far, and was impressed. I imagined that, if only I were given the opportunity, I could probably run the John Rigby Grammar School much better than the present management team. What I had not actually measured was the extent of my own ignorance and inexperience. How easy to be omniscient when you don't take the responsibility; how facile to ask the questions with no consideration of the answers; how simple to run the country from the safety of the back benches; how foolish to assume one's own indispensibility. Passing the parcel is easy - until the music stops.

My second misjudgement was that of believing that no-one worked quite as hard as I did. Should the opportunity arise, I would be more than willing to inform anyone prepared to listen of my excessive work-load. I suspect that many of us, at that age, imagine that we are unique in our sense of commitment. Fortunately, the majority grow out of this tiresome habit, although it would appear that many of us in the teaching profession have an appetite for telling others of the unparalleled difficulties we face in the discharging of our duties. To some extent, this may be a justifiable response to the widely-held misperception that teachers languish in short working hours and long holidays, but it does convey the impression that teachers complain more than most about their jobs, perthaps because they feel unappreciated. I suppose that all jobs are harder than we imagine. I really have no idea how demanding it is to be a pub landlord or a midwife or a parking warden. All I do know is that it is a mistake to underestimate the demands of other people's occupations.

My self-satisfaction was unnecessarily encouraged further by a most favourable report from Her Majesty's Inspectorate when the school underwent a general inspection some time later. Ralph Jeffrey HMI, who inspected Maths and Art, gave me a morale-boosting appraisal. I cannot recall much of what he said, apart from a particular image he painted of the learning process. "You must remember that there are many ways of achieving objectives, particularly in art education," he told me. "You may have the same starting point and the same finishing point, but the journey between the two may follow different routes. It is rather like..." he made an oval gesture with hands and furrowed his brow, "let me see...er," his face lit up, "a lemon!" When John Mockett told me that Cardinal Allen Grammar School was facing a general inspection in about a month's time, I related this little episode to him. Thus, when HMI Ralph Jeffrey later described to John the methods of achieving objectives in art education, concluding with "It is rather like... let me see...er..." - pause; oval gesture; furrowed brow - John casually suggested "A lemon?"

So, everything ran smoothly in 1966 - the car, the job, the self-belief. Maturity would later bring a more substantial confidence; one that did not require the kind of reassurance that complacency invites. There would no longer be the need to accelerate from traffic lights more rapidly than anyone else; there would be strength in the concealing, rather than the revealing, of the hours one worked.

The author playing one of his collection of harmoniums

My Cortina GT 'Police Car' (see p.98)

BOYS' HOBBIES

Towards the end of my Art School days I bought a guitar. It was rather battered and cost me £3, which was probably more than it was worth. I had decided to take the lazy route to guitar-playing by removing the top string and tuning the instrument to a tonic major chord. This meant that I could produce almost all of the necessary chords for country, folk and rock 'n roll music without having to learn complicated fingering. Quite quickly I learned to play majors, minors, suspended fourths and G-sevenths. Inspired by this rapidly-achieved success, I went to the music shop on Tulketh Street in Southport, bought the bottom string of an electric bass and put it onto my guitar. As I tightened this huge string, disaster struck as the guitar folded in the middle with a series of dramatic cracking sounds. I was mortified! How could a string possibly break a guitar? Well, it probably wouldn't have broken one in reasonable condition, but I had been playing an antique.

The next job was obviously to take my musicianship much more seriously and buy myself a brand new guitar. This transformation proved worthwhile and some of the efforts, to me at least, actually sounded half decent, particularly when performed in front of the wardrobe mirror. My repertoire expanded although, unfortunately, the recordings made on my reel-to-reel tape recorder did not sound quite as polished as I had expected them to be. Still, I was able to knock out reasonable renderings of 'Sweet Little Sixteen', 'Heartbreak Hotel' and 'Love Me Tender'. My pièce de resistance was 'Are You Lonesome Tonight?', even better than my David Whitfield impressions in the mid-fifties. The only factor holding me back was the tendency for strings to break at the most romantic and moving points in slow ballads, which tended to shatter the emotional mood I had worked so very hard to create.

When the Beatles took over the leadership of popular music, I went to Frank Hessy's in Liverpool and bought an electric guitar. It was a Les Paul copy and looked more expensive than the £22 I paid for it. Once again, the electric bass string was added and the top string removed, but I now had the advantage of playing though an amplifier, which gave my next-door neighbours as much anguish as it gave me pleasure. I couldn't fathom how to play the opening chord of 'A Hard Day's Night', but I did manage to master most of the songs in the film, my favourites being 'If I Fell', the introduction of which took me ages to learn, and 'I Should Have Known Better'. These and other Beatles numbers went down well at drunken parties when everyone wanted to sing their heads off into the small hours, and it was really quite amazing to hear how dramatically alcohol improved our voices. One of the main problems was that of losing the plectrum in the darkness, meaning that I had to use my fingers, which

84

invariably ended up covered in blood at the end of the session - blood shed for the sake of art.

The main problem of guitar ownership is that you tend to take the damn thing everywhere with you, and this results in people being bored rigid by your cheerful willingness to perform in response to the very slightest encouragement. Initially, you refuse to play and demean your own ability, but you allow yourself, with the greatest reluctance, to be persuaded in the end. The good news, for me at least, was that all this later prompted me to start writing and recording original music, despite the fact that I could neither play nor sing to any distinguished level. That activity, though, will be a story for a future occasion.

In the mid-1960s I started to collect wall clocks, although I cannot now recall quite how or why this hobby began. I visited a number of antique shops throughout the north-west in my search for bargains because, in those days, it was possible to buy quite a handsome piece for about £10. Most probably in pursuit of the instinct that had attracted me to customise cars, I painted these clocks as a means of adding some individuality to their appearance, sometimes adorning them with paste jewellery, which proved particularly effective when attached to the pendulum. I suppose the main attraction lay in the fact that they moved and they made a sound, giving an active presence - a life of their own. Within a few years, the cost of these clocks increased considerably, for there opened up a market for them in Japan and America, and it was then that I found the hobby had become too expensive.

I then turned my attention to harmoniums and American organs, the difference between them being that one sucks and the other blows, although I cannot now remember which is which. They were quite cheap - often only about £5 - mainly because many families were glad to get rid of them. The opportunites for customising were unlimited and one of my particular favourites ended up with the white keys being painted green. My great joy was playing Bach's Toccata in D minor - actually C minor in my case - but only the first sixteen bars because that was all I could master. The hobby ran out of steam when I acquired my fifth organ, simply because there was nowhere to keep them. As it was, there were two in the front room and three in the garage, and I was finally forced to give them away to anyone willing to collect them.

I suppose that my interest in collecting organs was inspired, to a large extent, by my friend John Mockett. He played a real organ - three manual and pedal - at his own church, St Joseph's Anderton, and could perform on even grander instruments, given the opportunity. Talented as he was, he always played from music, and once told me the tale of a problem he faced when his music disappeared. He was fourteen years old and had

85

just taken over duties at St Joseph's from a lady who wanted to retire. He was in the middle of playing a piece during Communion when the manuscript started to curl over at the top. John's hands were fully occupied and so, in order to avoid the sheet falling onto the keyboard, he butted it with his head. That was the age when he wore Brylcreem, which caused the manuscript to stick to his hair. He bravely continued playing, whilst shaking his head vigorously to free the music sheet. Inevitably, as the paper broke free from his hair, it took flight from the organ loft and flew down, stalling in a series of upward curves, and onto the congregation. Somehow, he managed to finish the piece from memory.

Although it was not really a hobby, I should mention a pastime John and I enjoyed whenever I visited him before going for a drink at the Grey Horse. It sounds disrespectful, I know, but we used to go into hysterics at some of the 'In Memoriam' messages he would read to me, in his finest Lancashire accent, from the current issue of the Chorley Guardian. We were particularly amused by verses that didn't scan, such as:

We really missed you, Dorothy,
When you just walked out of the door.
We cannot quite believe that we
Won't ever see your happy smiling face around here any more.

Another that stayed in the memory was:

Just when his hopes were greatest; just when his life was best,
God came down and took him to his eternal rest.
In memory of Albert Longbottom, aged 97.

John also used his power of mimicry when reading articles to me from the Catholic Pictorial in a perfect Liverpool accent. He chose reports of Primary School Football matches, a typical extract being:

Our Lady of the Assumption put considerable pressure on St Francis of Assisi in the first half, but the second session saw increasing penetration from St Francis, with Our Lady hanging on grimly and in danger of cracking under the onslaught. In the end, the pressure told as Our Lady's defence collapsed, and St Francis, looking ever more menacing, won just rewards for consistent attacking. However, praise should be offered for Our Lady's courage in the face of adversity, and to St Francis for perseverance.

The final hobby of the 1960s was wine making, conducted the lazy way by buying tins of concentrate from Boots in Chapel Street. At the peak of this activity, I had ten demi-johns fermenting away in the garage, most of them looking like urine samples from a medical laboratory, and tasting very little better. I remember taking all this very seriously by keeping highly detailed lists of the ingredients, the exact dates of starting, the introduction of finings, the colours of bottles, the designs of labels, and so on - another example of my obssession with lists. I'm bound to concede that the

John Mockett at the organ of St Joseph's Anderton

One of the wide corridors of Upholland College

87

administration was rather more impressive than the results, and I imagine that the wine connoisseurs of the day might well have described my products as having "an unmemorable character with a slight suggestion of nausea in the aftertaste".

The truth is that, increasingly over the years, my work had become my main hobby. People might say "you should get out more," and they would be right to do so. This kind of close involvement with one's chosen occupation represents both good news and bad news. The good news is that it is possible to see projects through to the very highest possible level of quality without bothering to count the time spent, even if it means working into the small hours and at weekends as well. The bad news is the same as the good news.

BOY FATHERS

In September 1966, Father Cheetham, Headmaster of Upholland College, made contact with me to ask if I would do some part-time teaching of O level Art in the early evening to boys at the Junior Seminary. This would be for one session per week from 5.30 to 7 pm and, although the pay he offered was modest, it was convenient for me to make a call there on my way home from Orrell. On the first occasion, I was invited to take tea and toast (and honey) with the priests at five o'clock. This was a most friendly gathering around an enormous rectangular table in the dining room, and I found it such a pleasant experience that I made sure it preceded my evening lesson every Tuesday.

The priests I remember meeting at that time were Fr Forshaw, Fr Gaine, who is now Dean of my area in Birkdale, the young Fr Alger, and the most senior member of the College, Monsignor Breen, whose grand-nephew David was then a pupil at the Cardinal Allen Grammar School in West Derby where my friend John Mockett taught. The College itself was a vast building with corridors that would have been large enough to divide into sizeable rooms. The grounds were beautiful, with large rhododendron bushes surrounding the lake.

The boys were a joy to teach, such was their enthusiasm, and many of them were clearly quite disappointed when the bell sounded to end the lessons. I imagine that being taught by a layman was something of a novelty, even though the atmosphere created by the priests in the 1960s was considerably less formal than it would have been in an earlier time. In the academic year that followed, I was asked to teach A level Art and, in 1968-9, A level General Studies. I was flattered by the presence of a few priests in some of my lessons. Evidently, they came along because a number of the older boys had told them how much they enjoyed the subject, a rare achievement, as anyone who has taught General Studies will be aware.

88

The uncertainty I felt at Upholland concerned the age of the boys who were there, some of them as boarders from the age of only twelve. Although I, myself, had boarded at eight, it was not then associated with a vocational aspiration, as it was with those at the College. There was a suggestion amongst some members of the Catholic laity that younger boys who trained for the priesthood did so more on the strength of their mothers', rather than their own, vocations. I have no idea how true this might have been, and it does strike me as rather cynical. Nevertheless, the setting of young boys on a life-dedicating career path of this nature does raise doubts, and I am sure that the senior staff at Upholland were aware of them. Over a period of time, the status of boys in the seminary changed from that of training for the priesthood to one where, at a certain point in their young lives - perhaps at eighteen - a priestly vocation might emerge. Thus, the decision was postponed until those who made it were mature cenough to do so with confidence and understanding.

Teaching at St Joseph's College, Upholland really was a joy, badly remunerated as it undoubtedly was. When I left John Rigby in 1969, Brian Lewis took over my class, and David Town, a colleague of John Mockett's and subsequently of mine, also taught Art there. I cannot remember a time in my teaching career when the pupils displayed stronger motivation or greater pleasure in learning than here, and I treasure the memories of this unusual and gratifying experience.

PART THREE

WHAT'S LOVE GOT TO DO WITH IT?
1967-69

THE FRENCH CONNECTION
SYSTEM
ALL YOU NEED IS LOVE
THE FOOL ON THE HILL
IS LOVE ALL YOU NEED?
PERFORMANCES
UPWARD MOBILITY

19671967196719671967196719671967

THE FRENCH CONNECTION

At the beginning of the new academic year, the Modern Languages department at John Rigby acquired a new resource - a French Assistante. Her name was Anne-Marie Meslin and she came from a village called Saint Aubert, near Cambrai in northern France. During that year-long stay in England, she lived in Ormskirk Road, Pemberton, at the home of the Hardman family. Mr and Mrs Hardman were the parents and next-door neighbours of my good friend Barbara Warren, wife of Stan and mother to a succession of John Rigby boys: Nick, Phil, Stephen, Timmy and Andy; daughter Kate being a pupil at Wigan Convent. This was a warm, busy and amusing family whose company and hospitality I enjoyed greatly.

Right from the start, Anne-Marie and I formed a friendship which developed into a closer relationship as the year progressed. She was something of a perfectionist who approached her teaching duties most conscientiously, and she soon became a valuable member of staff. I got less opportunity to use my rusty A level French than I would have wished, for she insisted that one of her objectives during the stay was to improve her English, which we tended to speak both professionally and socially, as well as romantically. She was a good sport, and she had to be to put up with the unceasing staff room banter, all of it in good nature of course.

In the later part of that academic year, two young French boys, Olivier and Philippe, attended John Rigby for two weeks and, like Anne-Marie, were hosted at the Hardman's. One mid-day break, Olivier was playing cricket with some of the boys on the school playground when he was hit on the bridge of the nose by the ball. Blood gushed out, and he was clearly in some distress, and so I carried him to the medical room where I attempted to administer first aid. Two blue marks on the upper part of the nose suggested that it was broken and, believing it was safer to assume the worst, I put him into my car, having sent for Anne-Marie to accompany us to hospital. It was bad enough to sustain injury without having a language problem into the bargain.

As we arrived at Wigan Infirmary, I parked the car as near to Accident & Emergency as I could, so that we could get immediate attention for Olivier. Before I could get out of the car, a small and irritable man with a peak cap and a jacket, covered with brass buttons and ostentatious epaulettes, rapped on the driver's window, which I wound down. "Yer can move this vehicle from 'ere fer a start!" he shouted. I opened the door, pushing him backwards, and carried the bleeding Olivier into reception, totally ignoring the officious oberführer of the car park. We very soon discovered that an operation would be necessary and, coincidentally, that the boy's father was himself a surgeon. I was so glad to have Anne-Marie there to make the phone call to France and to obtain verbal permission for surgery to take place. As I left Wigan Infirmary, leaving Anne-Marie to stay with Olivier, the car park attendant gave me a forbidding scowl and, judging from his facial expression, probably put a curse on me as well.

In the summer of 1967 I had bought my first cine camera, an Eumigette Zoom,using the new Super 8mm format. I am quite unable now to

The author and Anne-Marie Meslin outside John Rigby School

Timmy Warren in the film 'The Watch', set in Rivington

remember what prompted this purchase, but I do recall being captivated by the entire process of film making almost immediately. Of course, there was no instant gratification in those days, for there was a two-week wait for the film reel to arrive back from processing before you could see what you had taken. The excitement of the yellow package dropping through the letter box was considerable, although it was sometimes shortlived when the entire four minutes turned out to be black or, at least, too dark to use, as could happen on rare occasions.

My first effort at a simple production was entitled 'The Watch'. It was set in Rivington - still one of my favourite Lancashire areas - starring nine-year-old Timmy Warren as himself and Anne-Marie as the ghost. It was a fairly uninspiring story: 'Boy explores ruined castle and finds pocket watch; ghost frightens him; he runs away to safety amongst oriental gardens; he examines the watch once again; ghost reappears; boy runs for his life; End.' Timmy ran beyond the point of exhaustion for the sake of the film, and Anne-Marie did her best to look frightening, although the wearing of my academic gown back-to-front over her head was rather less terrifying than Timmy's screams implied. I did not know it then, but this was the beginning of a continuing and fulfilling involvement with the moving image.

As the time for Anne-Marie's return to France approached, we became still closer than before, and there was quite clearly the chance of an engagement in the future. I decided to drive her to London, in order to make her journey more agreeable. We broke our journey in Derbyshire so that I could show her Alderwasley Hall, where I had been a boarder from the age of eight to eleven. This was a revelation to her, never having seen an English Prep School, and a nostalgic return for me as I paid my first visit there since leaving in 1949. There were few people around, for they had broken up for summer, but we did meet one of my old teachers, Mr Reilly, my favourite. He had now retired and lived alone in a small, unkempt caravan in the school grounds. I think he got more pleasure from our meeting than I did, for I was deeply saddened by witnessing his humble existence and the degree to which he had aged since last we met. Quite inevitably, he later died alone in the caravan.

Anne-Marie wished me a tearful goodbye from the window of the train at Victoria Station, and I think that was the moment I wondered if I was cut out for marriage. I was twenty-nine, which meant I had spent a number of years as a young adult cultivating independence and the freedom it gives. As a consequence, I had probably become more selfish than I realised, and I knew Anne-Marie well enough to understand that, with her, I could not readily combine being a husband with being a bachelor as some men, including my brother, had managed to do.

92

In Summer 1969, I stayed with Anne-Marie and the Meslin family in Saint Aubert as part of a holiday in northern France. I think it was then that I got cold feet and decided that, when in doubt about cementing our relationship, it was easier to do nothing. In the end, Anne-Marie married a good Frenchman called Bernard and eventually became the mother of five children. Thankfully, we are still in touch with each other today but, at that point at the end of the 1960s, I had unwittingly committed myself to the status of a single man.

SYSTEM

By 1967 there was a range of clubs and societies in the school, but some of them met only on a spasmodic basis. I discussed with Tony Hilton, Alec Hurst and Paul Berkeley-Jones the possibility of combining these various activities into one umbrella organisation which would meet on a regular basis for one evening per week after school. So it was that System was formed, incorporating many different societies, almost all of which met from 4 pm to 6 pm on Friday evenings. Boys were asked to pay five shillings per year to join System, and this offered them the chance to take part in as many of the activities as they wished.

The Art Society had been running already for six years, the 3-D Group, catering for those who enjoyed making three-dimensional art, for four, and Typo, a small and enthusiastic group of printers with their own little room that was papered on walls and ceiling with font broadsheets, for three. The Film Set was new, but the Wargames Society, a popular activity started by Tony Hilton, was already well established after only twelve months of life. Rita Smith, assisted by Pat Heenan, ran the Drama Group, which put on a number of productions, including 'Noah's Flood' with Chris Riordan as God, and an extract from 'A Man for All Seasons', with the part of Thomas More being played by Peter Coulson. There was also Micro-Theatre, an activity involving puppets.

Alec Hurst ran the Basketball & Gym Club and Stephanie Palin introduced cookery with the 'Cours de Cuisine'. Other activities included clubs for Judo, Sailing, Bridge, Chess, Go, Table-Tennis, Subbuteo, Golf and Stamps, as well as the History, Polish and Literary & Philosophical Societies. There was even a minibus service for boys who would otherwise have difficulty in getting home without the school bus, and Paul Berkeley-Jones bravely offered to be the regular driver. The main reason that System worked was because it met on a regular basis and was never cancelled.

At the end of each session, Tony, Paul and I, along with any others who wanted to join us, would meet in 'The Old Engine' at Kitt Green for 'Chicken in the Basket', something of a novelty in the 1960s, washed down with pints of bitter or schooners of sherry. I recall one Friday when, after a long day's work followed by System and quite a large amount of alcohol, I drove home in a state of fatigue with the clear image of two sets of white lines down the middle of the road. It was my first taste of double vision at the wheel and, although it was long before breathalysers, it frightened me into never repeating the experience.

There was another occasion when, after System had finished, Tony Hilton, Harry Finch and I went for a drink at 'The Saracen's Head' in Standishgate. I was tired, Harry had a headache and Tony had an upset stomach. I went to the bar and ordered a half of shandy and a tomato juice for Harry and me. "What's the third one having?" asked the landlord. "Nothing", I replied. "You can sod off!" he told me, and we trooped out of the pub in dismay. The following evening, my friend Kevin Sharkey asked the landlord why he had refused drinks to three of his friends. "I don't serve poofs!" he retorted.

ALL YOU NEED IS LOVE

Those who refer casually to the 'Swinging Sixties' are in danger of giving the impression that the entire decade was characterised by a consistent international movement for change driven by young people with common aims. It wasn't. The difference between 1961 and 1969 was at least as great as that between the sixties and the seventies in terms of people's outlooks and expectations. Some have forgotten, or perhaps never knew, that the 1960s ended in a mood of some disillusion, not least as a result of the mounting discontent of young people with the Vietnam War and other products of American and Soviet expansionism. Protest was vigorous and often violent. One redeeming aspect was that it was generally driven by ideology rather than by anarchy. It is generally easier to forgive most actions when they are purpose-driven.

Before things turned sour, they turned sweeter. In 1967 there was what was called 'The Summer of Love', and the Hippie Flower Movement, which originated in San Francisco and spread rapidly throughout America and Europe, capturing the imaginations of many young, and some not so young, people. It was underpinned by a rejection of modern society's materialistic values, and believed in 'dropping out'. The influences were widespread. The encouragement of the Harvard University psychologist Timothy Leary to 'tune in, turn on, drop out' was one of many slogans designed to inspire rejection of the status quo and the embracing of the new drug culture, in particular the psychedelic (mind expanding) substances, such as LSD - known as 'Acid' - which Leary himself manufactured and distributed. In popular music, Bob Dylan caught, and shaped, the mood as well as anyone.

At the beginning of the year, ten thousand people attended the 'Human Be-in' in San Francisco, with the message: "Don't be afraid, come on out and *be*, be who you really are". If this now sounds rather daft, it is arguably far less harmful than the wave of cynicism that has since swept over much of today's society. Perhaps it is preferable to be an impractical optimist than a carping misery. Much better to believe that 'anything is possible' than to assume that 'nothing matters'.

At this time, it was probably much more fun to be a teenager than a parent; no doubt it always was. With many new ideas permeating fashion, music, technology, art, entertainment, hairstyles and other aspects of contemporary life, there came the newly-found will to mount a challenge to authority figures in general, and to parents in particular. Customary deference was fast going out of fashion, and those parents who wished to appear enlightened, on the one hand, and influential, on the other, were faced with the unenviable dilemma that successive generations of parents have inherited. The roots of all this most probably grew in the hothouse of Rock 'n Roll about twelve years before. It established a desire in the young to embrace culture that their parents and other adults simply could not stomach - too big, too loud, too colourful, too rude. Much popular music at this time was disagreeable to the older generation. The exception was The Beatles, who managed to appeal across a wide age-range as none had done before, and very few have accomplished since.

'Sgt Pepper's Lonely Hearts Club Band' was widely believed to be the best that The Beatles achieved. It came between 'Revolver' and the White Album, and most clearly demonstrated both their creative talent and their versatility. Almost all of the songs and, most certainly, the cover design by Peter Blake, broke new ground, and it was widely believed that 'Lucy In The Sky With Diamonds' was written to advocate the use of LSD. The claim that this album was the turning point in the writing of popular music is not strictly accurate. I have always felt that the real change agent was 'Strawberry Fields Forever', and that the producer, George Martin, deserves at least as much praise as members of the group for this significant progression. The album was quickly followed by the single, 'All You Need Is Love', which both mirrored and influenced the prevailing youth ideology.

In truth, we all needed far more than love, but the message was seductive, and it would certainly do for the time being. Better to be loved, even if you did look like a Christmas tree. Hair became longer, trousers tighter - but only at the hips - dress was flamboyant and brightly coloured, and headbands and lovebeads were worn. In Chelsea's Kings Road or in Carnaby Street it was impossible to shock anybody by your appearance. In Market Square, Wigan, or in Chapel Street in Southport, it was a different matter, at least for a few years yet. For all the extravagant colour of the period, the vast majority of people in Britain were still watching their television programmes in black and white.

By now, there was an increasing influx of working-class kids into the universities, almost all of them the very first in their familes to be educated beyond the school leaving age. As well as reflecting a growing expansion in educational opportunities, this symbolised a new freedom for young people from ordinary backgrounds. Freedom was expressed in other ways, such as 'free love', which cut across the already widely-broken rule that sex before marriage should not take place. It wasn't that these youngsters were the first to indulge in pre-marital sex; it was that they were the first who were not ashamed to admit it. As with all freedoms, there was a price to pay: an increase in teenage pregnancies; the growth of single-parent families; a demand for back-street abortions. Customarily, people blamed television, and those who didn't blamed comprehensive education. At the beginning of the year the Society for the Protection of Unborn Children was formed. Six months later abortion was legalised.

One of the offshoots of an increase in freedom was a comparable increase in political radicalism, much in evidence at universites, and nowhere more so than at Berkeley, California, the Sorbonne in Paris and the London School of Economics. By the late sixties, many universities were overcrowded, for the steady increase in numbers had not been matched by building expansions, and the resulting congestion was undoubtedly one of the factors leading to alienation within the student body. Also, as the media became more internationally oriented, issues in one country could attract interest and action in another. Thus, the Vietnam War and the Civil Rights Movement in the USA fired the imaginations of young people in Britain too. Within this climate, it was hardly surprising that the fastest growing degree course in the universities was Sociology.

This was the year that saw the start of Radio One, a rather late response by the BBC to the discernible demand for pop music radio that the pirate stations, such as Radio Caroline, had been supplying. A clear sign of the change in the lives and outlooks of children was shown in the demise of 'The Boy's Own Paper' after 88 years of publication. The year was also marked by the world's first heart transplant, performed by the South African surgeon, Dr Christiaan Barnard. Celtic became the first British football club to win the European Cup, and Manchester United were Division 1 champions, enabling them to match Celtic's achievement one year later. Brian Epstein, the Beatles' manager, died from an overdose, and Che Guevara was executed in Bolivia at the age of thirty-nine. The Metropolitan Cathedral of Christ The King was consecrated in Liverpool; homosexuality was decriminalised in the United Kingdom, and Engelbert

Humperdinck was at number one in the pop charts for about six weeks with 'Release Me'. Well done, Engelbert! We preferred Procol Harum's 'Whiter Shade Of Pale', which I first heard on the coach radio during a John Rigby Fourth Year art trip to Coventry Cathedral.

One of the finest givers of love I have encountered came into my life at about this time. I cannot now remember quite how we discovered her, but my mother and I found that we had a distant relative, an elderly nun who was a member of a Belgian order, the Sisters of the Little Ones. Her name in the order was Sister Madeleine - although we knew her as Auntie Lucy - and she had moved to Clumber Lodge in Victoria Road, Freshfield, to continue her work of caring for young unmarried mothers. She rejoiced in her calling and was probably the most unselfish person I have ever met. Whenever we took her presents, we knew that they would end up as gifts to someone else, for Sister Madeleine had no interest in material possessions and was totally devoted to the offering of support and love to these young girls and their babies. Her dedication to duty and the impressive strength of her faith were nothing short of inspirational.

In July, I came to the end of a five-year stint as form master of 5C. Over a period of ups and downs, and laughter and tears, we had got to know each other well and, on a general level, rather fondly. On the very last morning, they presented me with Benson & Hedges King Size cigarettes, but followed it up with an unexpected item. It was an engraved plaque bearing the words: 'To Mr P Bagshaw - Form Master of all 5C - 1962-1967'. I was so surpised by their kindness that I remained speechless for a moment, and then simply said, "Well, thank you. I'm lost for words". "Now, that's a bloody change!" replied Joe Wallace.

For me, the saddest occasion of all came towards the end of the year. Alan Cullen had been a member of my form over that five-year period. He was from quite a humble background and not particularly academic, but he had passed the eleven plus and was doing his best to keep up with the work. He came on one of my Lake District outdoor pursuits trips, and I suspected that it was his only holiday that year. I think he appreciated being at a grammar school, although he was too shy to say so, and he was just the kind of boy who was likely to derive benefit from being given the chance to exceed normal expectations. I liked him. He died as the result of a motorbike accident, and we attended his funeral in Wigan only a few months after he had completed his time at John Rigby. There is nothing more sad than the death of a young person, but those who work in schools know that they will face this sort of anguish from time to time. The other two boys who died in my time at the school were John Salisbury who was killed in a road accident, and John Johnson who died whilst on a seaside holiday.

1968196819681968196819681968196819681968

THE FOOL ON THE HILL

Armed with more confidence than was really merited by my first cinematic effort - 'The Watch' - I decided to embark on a major production at school. It was to be a modern re-enactment of the Stations of the Cross, dealing with the main elements of Christ's passion and crucifixion. This concept is something of a cliché today, but was slightly more original in the late 1960s. The two key pupils who worked most closely with me were David Lowe, a sixteen-year-old with a fascination with the film medium who acted as co-director, and Peter Hurst who played the major part of Jesus Christ, having no previous acting experience, either on film or on stage. Other boys either volunteered or were approached, and female parts were played largely by boys' sisters and friends from Wigan Convent. I was quite determined that no boy would appear in drag in *this* enterprise.

The working title for the film was 'Reach Out' because the theme music was initially planned to be 'Reach Out (I'll Be There)', with which the Four Tops had a number one hit in October 1966, but we later preferred 'The Fool On The Hill'. After David and I had worked out the beginning of the film, the first shoot was held at Gathurst Station down the hill from the school. Christ, having arrived by diesel train, was confronted by Judas and his followers, betrayed with a kiss, and bundled into a Police Car, which was actually my white Ford Cortina GT with a large Police sign (made out of a Hoover box) topped with a red flashing light, an authentic blue one being unobtainable. For some sequences, the car was driven by a member of the sixth form, Joe Killalea, and all went well until the car had to be parked halfway up Gathurst Hill so that we could take the next shot from the vehicle as it drove towards the school.

I had told the cast to run ahead of us and be out of sight as we swung into the drive where the title of the film, 'The Fool on the Hill' was displayed in two-foot-high letters across the front windows of the main building. I was just about to continue the drive when a car parked next to me on the hill, a most peculiar thing to do. As the driver wound down his window, I followed suit. "Playing at Policemen are we?" he asked with heavy sarcasm, unmistakable as a member of the Orrell CID. "Er, no, officer," I stuttered, "we're making a film". "Oh, making a film, are we?" I felt rather stupid and just nodded. With that, he and his colleague drove away, leaving David and me rather relieved that nothing further had been said. That night David Lowe studied a legal reference book in order to trace the offence we had committed. It was 'Impersonating a Policeman', and carried a range of sentences, according to gravity, up to and including that of imprisonment!

98

The author on camera and Peter Hurst as Christ during
'The Fool on the Hill' film shoot in Scholes, Wigan.

Jesus is crucified in the film 'The Fool on the Hill' in 1968
Co-director David Lowe is second from the left

A further much more serious problem confronted us one week later during the filming, at morning break, of Judas hanging himself. The plan was to place a dummy rope, attached to nothing, around his neck, whilst the real rope went under his armpits and across his chest, covered by a thick pullover. A group of boys were at one side of the main Art Room, and their job, when instructed, was to pull on the rope that stretched across the roof to Judas, who stood on a stool in front of an alcove. With hindsight, I should have asked a colleague to supervise the rope-pulling gang, rather than simply to send them an instruction with a pupil when action was required. We removed the stool, sent the message and filmed the 'hanging' of Judas. Unfortunately, the boys at the other end carried on pulling. To them it was probably a laugh; to me, and to the heavy Richard Riordan who played Judas, it represented a life-threatening emergency. David Lowe rushed around to the other side of the block whilst I held Richard up as high as I could, in order to reduce the pressure on his chest. As it turned out, no serious harm was done, but I was most certainly taught a salutary lesson that day.

After the trial and the release of Barabbas, the action moved to Scholes, a part of old Wigan that was in the process of demolition. This gave us an appropriately depressing backdrop and also ensured that we were generally away from spectators. The next sequence - and probably the most successful in the production - was the beating up of Christ, an activity we had chosen as a modern equivalent of the scourging. We discussed the procedures with the actors and decided that, for the sake of realism, they would actually have to hit Peter Hurst, albeit as lightly as possible. I was quite determined not to produce a film in which some of the most dramatic scenes would provoke laughter. The acting of the four boys involved, along with careful make-up techniques, assured the success of this section.

The Way of the Cross continued along Belvoir Street with St Catherine's Church in the background. The cross, itself, was made of scaffolding by my colleague, Kevin Sharkey, and was much heavier than it looked. Jesus was crucified on a hill at the edge of Porter's Wood next to the school. We dispensed with the crown of thorns in favour of a gnarled tree with similar characteristics. The trace of Christ's heartbeat was monitored on an oscilloscope, and the death was 'featured' on Granada News. Throughout the action, an eleven-year-old boy, played by Vincent Pickup, acted as witness to the action. At the finale of the film, he slowly raised a crisp to his mouth - a symbol of the eucharist - to the opening Marseillaise notes of "All You Need Is Love" by the Beatles, and walked away across the field. In the distance, the figure of Christ appeared and took his hand, signifying the resurrection. It all probably sounds corny today, but it seemed powerful at the time and was well received. Like most school enterprises, the taking part was probably of greater value to those involved than the finished product, yet I believe they shared the corporate pride many of us experience on these occasions, whether the activity is sport or performance or any group enterprise.

In May 2002, I decided to transfer the film onto video and to remaster it on computer and to enhance the sound. I fully expected to be amused by the naivety of this early production but, to my surprise, I was much more impressed by it than I had expected, so much so that I decided to make it available on video cassette to any of those who shared that experience in 1968. I was pleased, also, to be able to watch it over again with Peter Hurst, thirty-four years after he performed the role of Jesus Christ with such dedication.

This early experience of the making of movies was a revelation to me. I have no doubt that, had film studies been available as an option on my National Diploma Art Course in the 1950s, I should most certainly have chosen this in preference to Fine Art. Since that time, and throughout the process of using video both as an amateur and as a professional, I am happy to have found a medium which is right for me, albeit later than I expected. Even so, it is probable that my training in the visual arts of painting and drawing has transferred relatively painlessly to that of manipulating the moving image, and for that I am content.

IS LOVE ALL YOU NEED?

By the start of the year, the number of US troops in Vietnam was almost half a million. As the flowers were dying in San Francisco, the student protests around the world increased, encompassing not just America and western Europe, but several countries of the Eastern Block, Australasia, Canada, Japan and Mexico. The worst scenes were at the Sorbonne in Paris where many thousands of well-organised helmeted students overturned cars, threw petrol bombs and fought with the police, whilst huge numbers of trade unionists called a national strike in support of the students.

This was the year when Martin Luther King was assassinated, and 200,000 people were reported to have attended his funeral. Two months later, Senator Robert Kennedy, younger brother of the late President, was fatally shot. In this country, Enoch Powell made his 'Rivers of Blood' speech, and thereby stirred up racial controversy, inspiring some and disgusting others. On the following day he was dismissed by Edward Heath from the Shadow Cabinet.

In July, Pope Paul VI's Encyclical 'Humanae Vitae' prohibited Roman Catholics from using artificial contraception, although it probably succeeded in increasing the feeling of guilt rather than in stopping the practice. In August, the USSR invaded Czechoslovakia in order to topple

101

the liberal administration of Alexander Dubcek. Two months later, Richard Nixon was elected American President. 1968, then, was not the happiest year, and this was most probably the point at which the Sixties stopped swinging.

There was, on the other hand, some good news to raise my spirits. Manchester United won the European Cup, beating Benfica of Portugal 4-1 in the Wembley final. They were the first English club to achieve this distinction, and I languished in the delight of it all. The joy was enhanced by the fact that they had defeated the mighty Real Madrid in the semi-finals. Watching the game live on television with my good friends, the Edwards family, was a nerve-racking experience, particularly when the score was 1-1 at the end of ninety minutes, but the euphoria at the end of extra time was memorable. Although United had its customary defensive problems, the presence of Bobby Charlton and George Best - Denis Law being injured - guaranteed an incisive attacking approach. This was the perfect corollary of the Munich disaster ten years previously.

Two impressive films of 1968 were Stanley Kubrick's '2001: A Space Odyssey' and Lindsay Anderson's 'If'. In popular music, Cliff Richard didn't quite win the Eurovision Song Contest with 'Congratulations', an unknown Welsh girl, Mary Hopkin, sang 'Those were The Days', and The Beatles released 'Hey Jude'. None of these cheered us up in the way we needed, but The Scaffold put that right in December with 'Lily The Pink', quite the most intellligent song of the year. Taking groups camping could very well be described as a labour of love, mainly because the price of enjoyment was paid by much fortitude in the face of difficulty. In summer 1967, Kevin Sharkey, Alec Hurst and I organised a camping holiday in the Lake District for twenty boys from John Rigby. Anne-Marie had come over to spend part of the summer holiday in England, and I persuaded her to join us. The school had no camping equipment of its own at that time, and so I had to negotiate the loan of tents and other equipment from the Lancashire Education Authority's outdoor pursuits department. The tents were rather heavy, and the process of erecting them, with boys who had no previous camping experience, was a lengthy one. My obsession with the making of lists ensured that we took absolutely everything we could possibly need with us on the trip....except for butter and margarine, which I had stupidly forgotten to put on the list!

The camp was a great success, and all of the boys ended up more resourceful and self-sufficient by the end of their two weeks. For Anne-Marie this was a new experience, but she participated bravely in the rough and ready culture of camping. Of all of our activities, the most enjoyed was the cooking and eating of roast potatoes in the camp fire, although some of the burnt offerings were only barely edible, containing far more 'roast' than 'potato'. The following year, Kevin Sharkey, Maurice Glynn and I took a relatively small party of about eight to Yarrowford, not far from Selkirk in Scotland. This was more relaxed, for the group was much smaller, and travelling in three cars, rather than being dropped off by coach, enabled us to visit Edinburgh and to cross the new Forth road bridge. Maurice showed unexpected talents by riding his bicycle backwards across the campsite and walking along Yarrow Water on stilts, both admirable skills, although it is hard to imagine when they might come in useful.

196919691969196919691969196919691969

PERFORMANCES

As part of System - the John Rigby Grammar School group of clubs and societies - we made several further film productions, one of which was 'The Tell-Tale Heart', based on the horror story by Edgar Allan Poe. The setting was Harvey House, the home of the Irish Christian Brothers next door to the school. Only four characters were featured in the production: the old man, the butler, the detective and the boy, and the production team consisted of just six people. Although the project was more modest than 'The Fool on the Hill', it had its good moments and was worthwhile for those involved.

One memorable incident occurred when the body of the old man had to be buried under the floorboards. Since Stephen Kitching, the actor who played this role, was unfortunately absent from school with flu, the young producer, Malcolm Webster, was forced to deputise for him. Alan Southworth, as the butler, successfully lowered the body through the hole and replaced the floorboards. Quite forgetting that Malcolm was still under the floor, we then began to discuss our next shot, and it was only his frantic banging on the boards that reminded us to release him.

The school's tradition of performing works by Gilbert and Sullivan continued, this time with 'HMS Pinafore'. As usual, we took great pains to produce scenery of the highest quality, yet never more than on this occasion when Kevin Sharkey and the Technical department built a superb ship's bridge, complete with with a mast and sail. Consistent with our plan to base the sets on a different colour each year, Brian and I chose yellow for this one, with a violet-blue harbour scene in the background. We had become accustomed to receiving applause for the set as the curtains opened, but the warm response of the audience on this particular occasion was the most enthusiatic so far.

The other musical performance that was becoming something of a tradition, and for which I was largely to blame, was the 'Entertainments Club', a noisy and brash end-of-term concert, a part of the System group of activities. Alf Mockett and his Beatles tribute group played 'Baby's In Black' and 'I don't Want To Spoil The Party', whilst Zoony, inevitably, sang 'Waltzing Matilda' to an audience whose resulting ecstasy was a little disproportionate to what they had heard. "Your taste in music is somewhat catholic, Mr Bagshaw," commented Brother O'Halloran. These productions, along with many other school activities and some examples of boys' creative writing, were featured in System's 'Introspect Magazine', an annual publication then in its second year.

UPWARD MOBILITY

Much as I had enjoyed driving my white Cortina GT, my head had been turned by a new, up-market model from Ford - the Cortina 1600E. The E stood for 'Executive', and was a transparent attempt to attract young men with ambitions, not just to attain success, but to make sure that it was on display. I suppose that I was as gullible as the next man, and so I drove over to Palace Motors on the Wirral to have a look at the latest model. It was dark green with black seats, a leather steering wheel, a short gear lever, spot lamps and sculptured racing wheels with low-profile tyres. Like the GT, it had a binnacle of instruments, but it had the additional attraction of a walnut dashboard, to underline the 'executive' image that I had found so seductive.

I was smitten, and I signed the necessary papers with no clear idea of how I could possibly afford the £26 per month I was now required to pay under the terms of the bank loan I had arranged. I left the GT, taken as a deposit, and drove home in the manner of a man who had just made his first million, rather than someone who was living well beyond his means. What I didn't know at that moment was that my earning power was soon to increase to the point at which my gleaming new purchase would become affordable after all.

One day in February, my friend Harry Finch, Head of Geography, showed me an advert in the Times Educational Supplement. It was for the position of Deputy Head at a new school in nearby Skelmersdale - St Richard's RC Comprehensive. "Why don't you apply?" he suggested. I had been so very happy and settled at John Rigby that, for the most part, I hardly ever looked at job adverts and, without Harry's question, I should probably not have known about this opportunity. After some thought, I decided to explore further, but I comforted myself that I would be most unlikely to get it, a sure sign that I really had no appetite to move from the known to the unknown.

I sent for an application form and further details of the post at St Richard's, discovering that the Head was Peter McLaughlin, father of Stanley, a boy I taught at John Rigby. Although this increased my interest in applying, I still felt that I would do well to make the shortlist. After all, I had experience of only one school, and that was with grammar school boys, yet this was a mixed comprehensive school. Furthermore, most of the successful applicants for deputy headships at that time were teachers of English, History, Maths or Science, rather than Art. Finally, I was just turned thirty-one, perhaps a couple of years too young. Two weeks later, a letter arrived inviting me for interview.

There were five of us at the interview in St Richard's Presbytery. Of the other four, one in particular gave the unmistakable impression that the job was already his, such was his air of self-confidence. He had taught at the school where Peter McLaughlin had been Deputy Head. If this man considered that his appointment was a foregone conclusion, he most certainly fooled me. As a consequence, I was more relaxed during the interview than might otherwise have been the case, and this certainly helped me to perform better than I might have done.

After the ordeal was over, the five of us waited and made polite inconsequential conversation, apart from the confident one who seemed to want to score points over the others even at this stage. When I was asked to return to the interview room, I don't know quite who was more surprised, him or me. Monsignor Barry, the Chairman, simply asked "Mr Bagshaw, are you still a serious candidate for this post?" "Yes," I replied, feeling dazed by what was about to follow. "Then I am pleased to offer you the position of Deputy Headteacher at St Richard's Comprehensive School. Do you accept?" "Er, yes...I do...thank you."

I drove back from Skelmersdale through Upholland to John Rigby at three o'clock in order to break the news to my colleagues. The journey was surreal, as though the car wheels were not quite touching the road. My exuberance was almost off the scale. I could hardly believe what had just happened. At that moment, I was naively unaware of what the role of a deputy head truly involved, particularly in a school that had not yet opened. It didn't matter. This was an abstract feeling of achievement. It was intoxicating.

I awoke the following morning at about 6.30 with a sickening feeling of tension and anxiety. For at least twenty seconds, I could not make sense of this condition, let alone imagine its cause. Then, I remembered. I had been appointed deputy head; I was to leave John Rigby. But why was I so unnerved? Did I not rejoice exultantly only yesterday? I was not able to answer these questions, any more than I could dismiss them. To the outside world I displayed pride in my new appointment; inwardly I was paralysed with doubt. Thankfully, these hauntings lasted only a few days, but their intensity had disturbed me, and the close juxtaposition of ecstasy and agony told me that I still had much to learn, not least about myself.

Brian Lewis and I enjoyed a pleasant restaurant dinner with the boys who had recently taken the A level Art examinations. This was a tradition we had begun a few years previously, and it worked very well for all involved. The last day of the summer term was an emotional one. We gathered in the staff room to say goodbye to those leaving, and Fred Bethell, who had worked at John Rigby for ten years and was now moving to Christ The King High School in Southport, was given a present from the staff. At the beginning of that academic year, the staff committee had passed a motion restricting presentations to those who had completed ten or more years at the School, although I had opposed it. As a consequence, Alan Almond's eight years and my nine ruled us both out of receiving from colleagues any tangible recognition of our service.

Over those nine years I had been fortunate to have worked with some first-class colleagues and I would mention briefly some of those who have not featured in my recollections so far. Bernard Topping, Head of Classics, was a fine schoolmaster and a gentleman, and I was honoured when Anne-Marie and I were asked to be his daughter's godparents. Of all the Christian Brothers, Brother Thornhill, known to the boys as 'Des', had the most genuine and affectionate nature. He was not a disciplinarian of the old school, yet his pupils behaved in lessons because they like him, and we did too. Over the years, I had many arguments with John Clayton, but I must say that there was no-one on the staff more effective in the classroom than he, and there are many who remain deeply in his debt for the passing of O level English. He deserved great respect.

My nine-year career at the John Rigby Grammar School, Orrell, was greatly enjoyed and richly rewarded. I thought so then and I think so now. It is difficult to imagine a more agreeable setting in which to spend the first year of a new profession. The school was in only the second year of its existence, the setting was peaceful and rural, the staff was relatively small, and the eldest pupils were barely more than thirteen years old. I was young, with an enormous appetite for the excitement and fulfilment of my new career. Over and above this, I was allowed an unprecedented degree of autonomy for much of the time. I was to discover that there were to be very many happy and satisfying experiences in other times and at other schools. What is sure is that none surpassed the joy of those first nine years in that exhilarating and optimistic decade, when, if we only knew it, fortune smiled on us all for a good deal of the time.

The most memorable song of 1969 was Frank Sinatra's 'My Way'. It was, and still is, an anthem for all those aspirational young people who are tempted to place a slightly higher value upon their own attainments than perhaps they should. Regrets? I've had a few, but then again, too few to mention.

Ford Cortina 1600E in Lyndhurst Road

The Renault 16, bought in 1970 to replace the written-off 1600E

PART FOUR

JOURNEY TO A FOREIGN LAND
1969-71

SOWING THE SEEDS
ENEMY AT THE GATES
SHOCKED BY EVENTS
MANY HAPPY RETURNS
TRAINS AND BOATS AND PLANES
FLYING TOO CLOSE TO THE SUN
ANOTHER CHANCE

196919691969196919691969196919691969

SOWING THE SEEDS

St Richard's had no building of its own in September 1969 - a new school being planned for Tanhouse in about three years time - and so we had to be accommodated in the buildings that later became Westbank Comprehensive School on the campus that also included Glenburn School. I had realised that starting a school from scratch would involve a great deal of work, but I had not anticipated the huge scale of the operation. Quite naturally, Peter McLaughlin, as the Headteacher, shouldered the major responsibility for this, and I was in awe of his talents. He had been Deputy Head at St Kevin's, Kirkby, and then a Headmaster in Swaziland, so his experience was considerable. He was also a man of many personal qualities - integrity, warmth, spirituality and wisdom. I, as the Deputy Head, and Angela Haimes, as the Senior Mistress, undertook a large number of the necessary tasks, and the three of us worked diligently without a break throughout the entire summer holiday period.

In an existing school there are opportunities to look at procedures and to make changes. In a new school, everything has to be established from the very beginning. If I thought that this would be easy, I was in for a surprise. Decisions had to be made about staffing needs, school rules, the curriculum, discipline, the use of rooms, the timing of the day, admission procedures, relationships with local primary schools, uniform, worship, extra-curricular activities, information packs for parents, furnishing and equipping the school, and many, many other matters. Also, there were staff to interview and appoint at Head of Department level and below.

Skelmersdale was a small Lancashire town. When it was granted development status, most of the locals were not particularly apprehensive, for they had not yet grasped the possibility that they could eventually be overwhelmed by about 40,000 new residents. The plans for this town were ambitious, and there was a determination to learn lessons from earlier projects such as Kirkby, where residential development had simply not been matched by adequate commercial, social and recreational facilities. Skelmersdale was supposed to avoid previous mistakes; it was planned as 'The New Jerusalem', and with the style of house development on the Tanhouse estate, it certainly looked the part when viewed from the by-pass. One of the planners' boasts was that residents would be able to walk from one end of the town to the other without crossing a road. This turned out to be a mixed blessing in years to come, for the underpasses necessary to fulfil the pedestrian plan made the possibility of mugging at least as great as any danger from road traffic.

St Richard's started with 57 pupils aged 11 to 13 on the first day of its existence, and additional boys and girls joined us at the rate of about four per week as families moved into the area, a number from Kirkby, where hopes had not been realised fully. I had designed a new school uniform, consisting of purple blazers with badges in a modern version of a Maltese Cross. These proved popular, but there were mixed feelings about the lilac ties, particularly from the Head of PE, Laurie Cook, who thought them rather trendy and slightly effeminate. In retrospect, I think he was right. There was a refreshing sense of optimism in the school, just as there was in the town, for we all felt part of a new beginning. One of the main incentives for growth was the arrival of industry. At this time, no-one anticipated the forthcoming world energy crisis, along with the soaring inflation and growing unemployment that it would eventually bring.

My starting salary as deputy head was £2,210 per annum, a large amount for someone of thirty-one in 1969, and the £26 per month I had been struggling to pay for the Ford Cortina 1600E was now manageable. Just a little harder to manage was the change of role I had undergone since leaving John Rigby. Because our small staff was not yet able to cover the entire curriculum, some of us had to take on subjects for which we were not trained. Having taught Art and Religion to grammmar school boys only six weeks previously, I was now teaching English, Social Studies, RE and Music to mixed classes of all abilities. The problem was not the teaching itself, but the exhausting amount of preparation required in unfamiliar subject areas, all on top of other duties. There were many occasions when I did not finish organising work for the following day until 2 am.

Discipline took on a new meaning. In my previous post, I had been responsible for establishing good order in my own lessons, although I did extend this influence from time to time, in order to make sure that my form were well-behaved in colleagues' lessons. As Deputy Head, the discipline problems I faced were those referred to me by other teachers, and it was one of these that first precipitated a need for flexing my muscles. One morning, a boy in the second year knocked at my door. When I asked him what he wanted he informed me that his teacher had sent him to me to be strapped. I asked him to wait outside my room and went to see the colleague concerned, who was an experienced man. "He disobeyed me and I will not allow that. This is why I sent him to be strapped," he told me. I somehow felt that I was being tested out. "By all means send me the problem," I replied, "but don't send me the solution as well. I am not here to carry out your instructions. If you really want the boy strapped, you can send for the punishment book and do it yourself." The problem did not arise again.

As with all small schools, and particularly new ones, there is a warm family atmosphere that cannot last forever, but which is precious while it does. That is what we experienced in those early days, and I think it would be true to say that almost all of the children really enjoyed coming to school. This, of course, made our lives more pleasant, although it did not make our tasks any lighter. One of the most welcome pieces of news was the receipt of a request from Keith Yon, a lecturer at Dartington College, to work for a year in a comprehensive school in the north-west, simply for the experience. He came originally from St Helena, and turned out to be a gifted and charismatic teacher of music and drama, which, as well as relieving me of music teaching duties for some time, also provided a stimulating performing arts environment for St Richard's children.

I formed a lasting friendship with Yon, as he preferred to be called. I remember that our shared love of music attracted us to the new Liverpool Metropolitan Cathedral to see a stunning performance of the Verdi Requiem. As we came out at the end, I noticed some glass on the road near to my car, and thought that I had better be careful not to drive over it. As we got nearer to the vehicle, I realised that the glass was part of my passenger window, and that a huge hammer-head was lying on the seat. Because it was a very warm evening, I had taken off my suit jacket and carelessly left it on the back seat. Never again.

1969 was the year that the troubles in Northern Ireland began to take off, and the start of significant American troops withdrawals from Vietnam, reduced both the frequency and the intensity of student protests. An indication of money values at that time was shown in the raising of the minimum wage for farm workers to £13 per week. By far the greatest gathering of youth that year was at the Woodstock Festival in America where 400,000 were reported to have attended.

Concorde undertook its maiden flight and, to the amazement of the world, men landed on the Moon. US President Richard Nixon, greeting the astronauts on their return, in formed them that "This is the greatest year in the history of the world since the Creation." Well at least that really put Jesus Christ in his place! Slightly less significant was the finishing of Mrs

Dale's Diary on radio, but television produced two ground-breaking series: Kenneth Clark's 'Civilisation' and Monty Python's Flying Circus. This latter programme caught the imagination of most of my age-group, and followed the tradition of surreal humour that had been pioneered by The Goon Show and 'Beyond the Fringe'. All of this might have caught our attention more strongly had we not been so heavily absorbed in getting St Richard's Comprehensive School off to a good start. Too much of work and not enough of play may make one dull, but it can also exact a higher price, as I was soon to discover.

ENEMY AT THE GATES

Just like every other morning, the children lined up on the patio outside the main entrance. Yet it wasn't like every other morning, for I had to ask one colleague to supervise the pupils entering the building and I was forced to find another to take Morning Assembly for me. The cause of the problem was, as far as I could tell, the start of a bout of gastro-enteritis and, because it worsened over the next hour, I had no choice but to drive home and to go straight to bed. Although I never usually called the doctor to visit me, I made an exception on this occasion. Dr MacDonald examined me, announced that he was unable to detect any gastric problem, and wondered if anything was worrying me. I was puzzled by his enquiry and assured him that everything was fine, aside from the diarrhoea. He decided to sign me off work for a week anyway, and I felt surprisingly relieved at his decision, although I had no idea why at the time.

As days went by my physical condition improved, but I experienced a growing feeling of panic as the day to be signed off and to return to work approached. My visit to the doctor's surgery confirmed what he had shrewdly detected the week before, and this time the two-week note bore the words 'anxiety state'. I felt stigmatised by this description, accurate though it might have been, and I now had to reconcile my palpable sense of relief with an increasing burden of guilt over what I considered to be my unauthorised absence, a term that schools are so ready to use about their truants. Although I was aware that the 14-day period must eventually come to an end, I had managed to buy myself some degree of safety from whatever had been haunting me.

Day by day the creeping anxiety increased, and it was all the more traumatic because the cause was still unfathomable. I began to experience panic whenever the doorbell or the telephone rang, and the only place I felt safe was in bed. I stopped using the car, mainly because I felt that someone who was off work should not be seen driving. On the few occasions I decided to walk up the road to the paper shop, I avoided eye contact with anyone I passed. Slowly, I was building up a psychological shield to

111

insulate myself from any form of relationship with the outside world. One morning, en route to the paper shop, I passed the milkman in his float, and I vividly recall the envy I felt at what I regarded as his unchallenging occupation. If only I were able to earn my living in such a relatively straightforward way. This was the first indication to me that the source of my nightmare was located somewhere in pressure of work at school, and that it was more than simple fatigue.

On my second visit to Dr MacDonald's surgery, I decided to ask him if I could see a psychiatrist. To me, this initiative represented no less than a compounding of my tangled web of deception, but there now seemed no way of turning back. I simply could not face anything, let alone a return to work. To my surprise, my doctor made the suggestion before I did and, with enormous relief, I concurred at once. He promised to make contact with Southport Infirmary and would let me know when an appointment had been made. He thought it might take about a fortnight. Knowing that I simply could not survive a further two weeks without expert help, I returned home, found the appropriate section in Yellow Pages, and phoned the Liverpool number of a psychiatrist whose name was the first on the list. It was engaged, and so I tried the one at the end of the list and spoke, not to a secretary, but directly to Dr Charles Vaillant of Rodney Street, who I later discovered to be a Home Office psychiatrist of some eminence. I felt fortunate that he was able to see me the following afternoon, but it was more likely that he recognised my need for immediate help. My belief that using private medical care conflicted with my egalitarian outlook was sacrificed on the altar of desperation.

The next day I took the train to Liverpool Exchange and a taxi to Rodney Street, passing Leece Street, up which I had walked so many times on my way to the College of Art ten years earlier. I recalled briefly, and somewhat painfully, the happiness of those days and concluded that life would never again be so carefree. If anything exemplified the relationship between depression and self-pity, this was it. I entered the Rodney Street residence and was shown into a well-appointed lounge by a kindly woman. After about ten minutes, Dr Vaillant came to escort me to his surgery. He asked me to tell him about myself and how I was feeling. I stumbled through a series of barely coherent explanations, after which he asked me to lie on a couch whilst he gave me an injection. The effect was almost immediate. I started to weep as I listed a lengthy series of personal shortcomings and inadequacies. He listened patiently to this dismal litany and then asked me to return to the chair. "If I am going to be able to help, you must stop expressing guilt," he asserted. "You are not a failure; you are ill and, until you accept that you are ill, I cannot treat you." I felt marginally reassured by this. Perhaps I was ill after all. Dr Vaillant then

112

gave me a prescription for anti-depressants and asked me to visit him again in two weeks time.

The medication did not appear to have any discernible effect, aside from making me feel drowsy and constipated. My concentration diminished to the point where I was unable to read even a short newspaper article, and both radio and television were equally unwelcome. The only real diversion from sitting passively in my chair was the taking of walks, and these usually occurred as the light was fading, so that I would be unlikely to meet anyone. More often than not, I chose to walk along Selworthy Road, a prosperous part of Birkdale, which had the advantage for me of being relatively free from pedestrians. On one occasion I visited Our Lady of Lourdes Church, but did not stay because I felt ashamed and, somewhat to my surprise, I was unable to find consolation in prayer. The darkness was closing in, and I began to denigrate former achievements. I had convinced myself that, not only was I now incapable of functioning, but that I had never really done so effectively in the past. Within this agenda of despair, there was simply no prospect for the future. For the first time in my life I learned the impossibility of finding any escape from mental torment. The condition was worsened considerably by an awareness of those who have undergone much greater pressures than I could possibly imagine, yet have coped with fortitude.

The two-week wait for my next visit to Rodney Street was over at last. Dr Vaillant recognised that matters had worsened since we last met, and suggested that I be admitted voluntarily to the psychiatric ward of Walton Hospital. Although I protested tearfully, I eventually submitted to his advice on the basis that there seemed to be no sensible alternative. The following morning, my bother Denis drove me to Walton, where I was allocated to a bed in O Ward. I found the atmosphere horrendous in the extreme and, within about four hours, I had called a taxi and was soon making my way back home by train in a state of unrelieved panic. It was clear that I was unable to settle anywhere and that, when the mind is disturbed, one's physical location is irrelevant.

On Christmas Eve morning I sat in the front room with the curtains drawn, listening to the second movement of Beethoven's G Major Piano Concerto. I was, no doubt, feeding off my own anguish; a self-indulgent means of 'enjoying' bad health. Then, for no reason I can recall, and still taking a course of prescribed medication, I went for a car drive. My precious Cortina 1600E had not run for six weeks, and clearly enjoyed the journey no more than I did. It was almost inevitable that the episode would end in disaster, and so it was that, after a violent and dramatic crash which wrote off the car, I awoke to find myself in Southport Infirmary with relatively minor damage, except to my neck which had suffered whiplash injuries. I had no recollection of the accident, and was both fortunate and relieved to learn that no-one else was hurt. My only memory from that day was that the radiographer who supervised my X-ray was Eileen Gaunt, whose family lived two doors from us in Lyndhurst Road. There was now no safe place of refuge for me, and that Christmas night in 1969 was the lowest imaginable point on the barren landscape of my despair.

'C'était pendant l'horreur d'une profonde nuit' - Racine

197019701970197019701970197019701970

SHOCKED BY EVENTS

At the beginning of the new year I made contact with Dr Vaillant and told him that, if he was prepared to treat me, I was willing to give hospital another try, simply because I could think of no alternative. Two days later I was admitted once again to O Ward and prepared for a course of electro-convulsive therapy - ECT. This method of treatment, known to the Ancient Romans, adopts the alarming process of passing electric current through the brain. It has since become less fashionable, yet there have been many cases of people with depressive illnesses being rescued by this method, although very few specialists knew quite why and how it works. One of the methods now gaining ground is TMS - Trans-Cranial Magnetic Stimulation - which requires no general anaesthetic and is generally regarded as less invasive than ECT, but this had not evolved at the time I was under treatment.

Over a period of a month I received four doses of ECT, all under general anaesthetic administered by injection. The immediate after-effects were severe headaches, which usually passed in a few hours, and considerable short-term memory loss, which probably helped more than hindered my recovery, despite giving me the embarrassment of forgetting completely the visits that friends and relatives had paid me a few days previously. During this period I was sustained by many people's kindness and patience, most notably my brother and sister-in-law - Denis and Jay, my good friends from Wigan, Kevin and Marie Sharkey, and also my headteacher at St Richard's, Peter McLaughlin.

Very, very slowly the depression began to lift and, with this, came a moderate increase in self-esteem. One sign of recovery was the reading of a newspaper for the first time in three months. Little by little, I started to make conversation with others in the ward and, by doing so, began to break down the obsession with 'self' that had built up since the outbreak of my depression in the previous November. It was very easy to become so absorbed in personal anxieties that the needs and concerns of other people remain completely unconsidered. This applied, not only to fellow-patients,

114

but also to my visitors whose concealing of their own worries in my presence led me to conclude that they had none. Although I did not recognise it then, I was beginning to accumulate life experiences that would enrich the sensitivity of future dealings with others, proving that many unanticipated benefits can arise from even the most awful conditions.

Towards the end of February 1970, I was discharged from Walton Hospital and sent home with a prescription for mild anti-depressants and instructions to visit Dr Vaillant once a fortnight. My cousin, the Hon. Mark Watson, offered to send me on a recuperative holiday to Malta, but I did not then feel ready to manage such a venture on my own. My Head, Peter McLaughlin, started to bring round to me one or two small items of school administration, in order to lead me back into the right frame of mind for a possible return to work after Easter. At last, I was able to consider the notion that my life was not completely ruined, and that there might even be a future for me in teaching after all.

MANY HAPPY RETURNS

Over the Easter holidays, I bought myself a new car - a silver Renault 16 - in anticipation of starting the move towards some sort of normality. After further discussions with Dr Vaillant and my boss, Peter McLaughlin, a provisional return to St Richard's was proposed. As the day approached, I felt my sense of apprehension increasing, and I feared that this might cause the abandonment of the planned re-integration. Then, on the Friday morning in question, chosen quite deliberately to provide the cushion of a weekend immediately afterwards, I made the journey to Skelmersdale at an average speed of no more than 25 mph. The thought uppermost in my mind was that, at all costs, I must not turn back.

As I parked the car, a number of pupils spotted me and ran over to greet me. This welcome, genuinely affectionate, helped me over the first hurdle. As I walked towards the main building, dozens of other children approached, expressing their pleasure at my arrival. But what would be the attitude of colleagues? I can remember distinctly nearly losing my nerve as I entered the main school building. The moment I walked into the staff room, the worst of my fears were instantly dispelled by everyone's kindness. All those who have been absent from work for an extended period will identify quite readily with this experience. It underlines better than anything how dependant we are upon the way that others perceive us or, more precisely, how we *think* they perceive us. Role Theory explains how easily self-confidence can be undermined by the conflicting expectations of colleagues, and how mistaken it is to determine our actions on the basis of pleasing others. Anyway, I had just re-entered the earth's atmosphere without burning up.

115

St Richard's had moved on considerably during my absence, driven by the efforts of a committed staff, and inspired by the energies of Peter McLaughlin, Angela Haimes, Laurie Cook and others. The small family atmosphere I had enjoyed in those early years at John Rigby was evident here, reflected in an easy and respectful relationship between teachers and pupils. Skelmersdale, itself, was expanding at some pace, and there was still a strong feeling of optimism abroad in the town. There was good relationship between St Richard's and the local Catholic primary schools, and a key figure in this was Father Mike McKenna, the young School Chaplain, today a senior member of staff in the Archdiocese of Liverpool.

Once I had overcome the apprehension of reconstructing a career that had been very close to ending in disaster, life became bearable again. By summer there was a return to the exhilaration and fulfilment that I had assumed would never again be a feature of my work in education. I started a group of extra-curricular activities under the name 'Strike', adapted from the St Richard's name, and based it very much on the model of System, which had been so successful at John Rigby. The staff supported a wide range of after-school activities, and the take-up of these by the pupils was widespread and enthusiastic. My own enterprises embraced wargames, filming and sound recording and, before long, we had produced both an EP and an LP, consisting mainly of Beatles and Tamla Motown songs performed by the children, mastered on the school Tandberg reel-to-reel tape recorder and pressed by Cam Records of Liverpool.

By the beginning of the Autumn term, there were three year groups in the school and the number of pupils had passed the 200 mark. I had taken on the coaching of the Third Year soccer team, which was a pleasant and rewarding task, even though they lost most of their games as a result of having only a small pool of players to pick from. A duty that came my way was the arranging of the Carol Service in the Arts Theatre. I decided that we would try part-singing in some of the Carols, but I recall that the results were characterised more by effort than by attainment. Never mind; we did our best.

For me 1970 ended much more successfully than it had begun. Not everything went as I would have wished, however, for the Tories won the June election and a woman called Margaret Thatcher, about whom we then knew nothing, became Secretary of State for Education. The age of voting was reduced from 21 to 18 and the country suffered the greatest number of strikes since 1926. The growth of Indian Restaurants was considerable - in 1950 there were six; in 1970 there were 2,000. The Beatles made a documentary film and an LP called 'Let It Be' and then, to no-one's surprise, broke up, each of them releasing solo albums. Paul McCartney filed a law suit against Lennon, Harrison and Starr to dissolve The Beatles on a formal

Optimistic faces from the early 1970s on St Richard's School brochure

basis. The most popular songs of the year were generally Motown-style - 'Band Of Gold, 'Tears Of A Clown' and 'I Want You Back', although it was Simon & Garfunkel's 'Bridge Over Troubled Water' that turned out to be more influential than most other records of the year.

19711971197119711971197119711971

TRAINS AND BOATS AND PLANES

Having run eight five-day London trips at my previous school, I was keen to repeat the experience for St Richard's pupils, and the party of forty-six children and four staff left Skelmersdale and boarded the train from Wigan for their visit to the capital on 2nd January, 1971. Once again, the accommodation was at King George VI Hostel at Holland Park, and the itinerary was similar to those I had planned for trips in the 1960s. As was customary, our first evening consisted of a river trip from Westminster Pier to Tower Bridge, taking in the sights on the way. The next morning offered members of the group a choice between the four large museums in South Kensington, followed by Trafalgar Square, Whitehall, Horseguards Parade, Downing Street and a long walk up the Mall to marvel at Buckingham Palace in the afternoon.

On the second evening we went to the Model Engineer Exhibition at the Seymour Hall. One of the attractions was a control-line aircraft that flew in a large circle and at considerable speed. There was a low barrier to prevent spectators moving too close to this exhibit but, because boys will be boys, one of our group, Anthony Topping, leaned too far forward, was hit on the side of the head, and briefly lost consciousness. An ambulance was called and I accompanied him to St Mary's Hospital in Kensington where they decided to keep him in for observation. I had the surreal duty of phoning his parents to tell them that their son had been hit by a plane, but that he was not seriously injured. Aware that he would feel rather isolated, I made sure to visit him before breakfast on the following morning, which extended a very long working day even further.

Most of the St Richard's pupils had never been to London, and I suspected that more than a few had not even travelled anywhere before without their parents. Partly because of this, they kept very close to the teachers for fear of getting lost, and their excitement and sense of wonder resembled that of much younger children. For all the marvels of the Imperial War Museum, Big Ben, the Natural History Museum and the Houses of Parliament, nothing surpassed the excitement generated by the pigeons in Trafalgar Square. The following picture is of a girl, whom I shall not name, dressed in her best coat and holding a new handbag bought specially for the trip. This image of pure joy still moves me.

St Richard's girl in Trafalgar Square on the 1971 London Trip

Some confusion was caused in Britain by the introduction of decimal currency in mid-February. For younger people, it posed few problems, but for the older generation there was a very long period of assimilation, and some never quite came to terms with it. "Why din't the wait fer all th'owd folk ter die off furst?" a old Wiganer might well have observed. The funniest story I heard at this time, but one which cannot be captured in print, was from John Mockett, who had been having a meal in a Liverpool restaurant when he overheard two old ladies asking a Chinese waiter to explain the new currency to them. John's inspired rendering of the resulting dialogue was hilarious.

Those who suffered under the savage unemployment of the 1980s may be surprised to learn that, in 1971, the 815,000 out of work was the highest figure since 1940. This was the year that Intel invented the microprocessor, although hardly anyone was aware of it, and those who were would have had no idea at all of the size of its subsequent influence upon today's world. Without doubt, the most depressing memento of 1971 was to be found in the list of Number One hits, which that year included "Grandad" by Clive Dunn, "Chirpy Chirpy Cheep Cheep" by Middle of the Road, and "Ernie (The Fastest Milkman In The West) by Benny Hill. No...really...it's true!

FLYING TOO CLOSE TO THE SUN

As the Spring Term progressed, I became more deeply involved with an increasing number of projects both within and beyond the school curriculum. Point Six Youth Club, a purpose-built facility on the campus, served the social and recreational needs of teenagers from Glenburn and St Richard's. It was open most evenings, and I often stayed on until quite late, dividing my time between school admin and visits to the club. As time passed I increased my input into Strike activities, whilst at home I was moving bedtime further into the early hours. By the end of the first half-term I had developed a pattern of going to bed at 2 am and rising four hours later. On a short-term basis, this is rarely harmful, but once it becomes routine, then a price has eventually to be paid.

My energy level at this time was quite extraordinary, and I found creative ideas coming into my consciousness at a faster rate than I was able to process or apply them. This behaviour illustrates clearly the fine line between obsessiveness and mania; the former an eccentricity, the latter an illness. In addition, there was an even more alarming problem. When deep depression had disabled me eighteen months previously, I had been aware of its presence - how could I not have been? This time, however, I was quite unaware that anything was wrong, apart from the realisation that I was regularly burning the candle at both ends.

In the late winter of 1969 I had been unimaginably low; now I was so high as to be almost off the scale. My mind was racing with plans and enterprises, and I was unable to stop myself either talking or working. This bizarre behaviour was recognisable to all, except one person - myself. That, without doubt, is by some degree the most frightening statistic of this personal disintegration. The three who witnessed the worst of the condition were my mother, who must have been very deeply affected, my cousin, John Howells, and my brother, Denis. It was Denis, in fact, who engineered my re-admission to Walton hospital by arriving at the house early one morning. I was in my dressing-gown eating breakfast when he told me that Dr Vaillant wanted to see me, but that there was no need for me to get dressed, for he would take me there in his car. With surprising gullibilty, I agreed.

When we arrived at the hospital, I was led to a room where Dr Vaillant sat at a desk with his assistant, Dr Christie. Two male nurses were also in the room and a small glass of yellow liquid had been placed on the desk. "Drink it," ordered Dr Vaillant. I was taken aback by his brusque manner. "Why?" I asked. "Drink it!" he repeated. At this point I became agitated. "You're making a mistake," I told him. "There really is nothing at all wrong with me!" "I shan't ask you again," he insisted, "Now, for the last time, Mr Bagshaw, drink the medicine." Almost in tears and still protesting, I reluctantly swallowed the contents of the glass which, as I later discovered, contained Largactyl syrup. I was then led into O Ward and put to bed in a state of despair, feeling like an innocent man who had just been convicted of a crime he had not committed.

I remembered very little of what was a stay of about six weeks in Walton Hospital over the Easter of 1971. Although quite a number of people came to see me me, I could not piece together either the sequence or the frequency of their visits, and I imagine that this is nature's protection at work. When I have asked my cousin and my brother to fill in the missing pieces of this jigsaw, they have both warned me that I should not ask, and that nothing at all would be gained by learning more than I have managed to recall.

The visitors I do remember were Peter McLaughlin - although how he found the time is beyond me - my mother, my brother and sister-in-law, Kevin and Marie Sharkey, and, to my surprise, a boy from St Richard's with his mother. The most significant visit was from Monsignor Barry, Chairman of St Richard's Governing Body. He spent the first two minutes asking me how I was, but I quickly formed the impression that he was not really listening to the answer. He then passed me a sheet of paper and asked me to read it. I went cold, for it was my letter of resignation from the Deputy Headship of the School. "We think it is for the best," he said.

I signed the letter because I felt that there was no alternative. Monsignor Barry did not hang about. Why should he? His mission had been accomplished and so he left. I sensed no understanding whatsoever in our brief discussion, not a hint of the compassion that it would surely have been reasonable to expect. It was just a piece of business, now completed. I sat there in desolation, convinced that I had signed away, not just my present post, but my career in the teaching profession. I tried my hardest to disguise my feelings, yet I have no clear idea why, for no-one at all was watching.

It is inevitable that, after a breakdown, one looks for explanations. There is a widespread belief that anxiety is determined by external causes and, in part, this is true. There is, however, another causal factor. It is that which resides within the personality; one that is harder to identify and, as a consequence, much more difficult to explain. There are often straightforward means of escaping from our environmental difficulties - changing a job, moving house, and so on, but internal problems are not so easily confronted for, try as we may, we cannot run away from ourselves. Those who attempt to alter the nature of their circumstances, such as the taking of a new job elsewhere in order to leave their anxieties behind, are quite frequently disappointed. If the problem is an internal one, they simply take it with them to another location and, worst of all, fail to draw the obvious conclusion.

In that purgatorial period after resigning my deputy headship, I had abundant time to contemplate the external determinants of my illness. As I saw it, the first probably started in the last two terms at John Rigby, when my self-imposed work level was unnecessarily high. The second was that of abandoning a summer holiday in order to prepare for the opening of a new school. The third would undoubtedly be connected to a change of role, for it is widely accepted that changing of an occupation is one of life's more stressful experiences. The final one was that of working obsessively and ignoring the need for adequate sleep. This symptom was likely to be an internal problem and, if that were true, it might well be one that I was powerless to change.

The crucial question was that of wondering whether I could return to stress-free operation by the adopting of more sensible life-management strategies, or whether I was doomed, by my personality, to repeat the episodes of dysfunctionality. The answer would take some time to be revealed, and would most certainly not emerge before this second volume reached its end. In 1959, Sylvia Hindmarsh, my Education Tutor on the Liverpool ATD Course, said "Remember, everyone, that you can learn as much from a failure as you can from a success". I dismissed this at the time. Would she be proved right after all?

ANOTHER CHANCE

After my discharge from Walton Hospital, I was pronounced fit to return to work, but with the proviso that I must undertake a role with much less responsibility than before. A meeting was arranged at County Hall in Preston, where I discussed with Keith Wood-Allum, a senior officer of the Lancashire Education Authority, my future employment possibilities. He told me that he had arranged an interview for me with Alan Barnes, Head of Ruffwood School in Kirkby, to explore ways in which I might be taken onto the staff as a super-numerary teacher. I have to say that Lancashire were most helpful to me at this time and, far from the faceless bureaucracy that everyone assumes, they were both supportive and understanding.

I drove out to Kirkby with some apprehension, in no way reduced when I saw the size of the school. There were a few short of 2,000 pupils and a teaching staff of 115, rather different from what I had been used to. Alan Barnes was a considerate man who welcomed me to Ruffwood and expressed the hope that he would be able to employ my talents to the school's advantage. "Although you have been ill," he observed, " I am well aware of your quality and of your past achievements." I found this comforting, even though my anxiety was only just below the surface.

Mr Barnes outlined a number of responsibilities I might like to consider - Careers liaison work, Pupil Counselling, or the monitoring of In-Service Training. Then he referred to a venture he had wanted to start for some time, but could not afford to staff - that of setting up and running a unit for junior pupils who were considered maladjusted (now an old-fashioned term). With the naivety I had been prone to exhibit on several previous occasions, I said "That last one appeals to me. It sounds like an interesting challenge". In the world of understatements, this was in the top ten!

My new Head appointed me, apologised for being unable to match my Deputy Head's salary, but offered me a Scale 2 Responsibility Post by way of compensation. I thanked him and assured him that money was the least of my present concerns, as indeed it was. He then took me down to one of the eight Houses and introduced me to Allan Paver, the Housemaster of Wedgwood, to which I had been assigned. Allan was both welcoming and kind, making me feel already part of the Ruffwood team by introducing me to staff in the houseblock. I immediately found that the openness and friendliness of my new colleagues did much to assuage my insecurity on that first afternoon in Kirkby.

The plan for my new role was that I should visit each of the eight housemasters and, on their advice, compile as list of about a dozen of the most problematic 12- and 13-year olds in the school, with a view to setting up a withdrawal unit. This group would spend the bulk of the week with me, but go off to other members of staff for science and for technical subjects.

This process produced a list of about twenty-five names, but when I counted those given three stars, in the style of a Which? report, the number was twelve. I then visited a number of subject teachers to seek advice and to borrow books and other material for use with this new group. Once again, they were co-operative, friendly, and most anxious to help - with just one exception. His manner was cool and he warned me that I should be sure to return the books as soon as I had finished with them. At that time, I could not fathom his attitude, but it is worth mentioning that he later turned out to be, not only a highly-valued colleague, but also the closest friend of all in my time at the school.

The staff of St Richard's insisted that I join them for an end-of-term drink at the Beacon Inn after school had broken up for summer. Any embarrassment I felt at this prospect was dispelled immediately by their good wishes and thanks for my contribution. Even though I *had* made a useful input to St Richard's, I nevertheless felt a little guilty, for my two prolonged periods of illness had not been exactly helpful to the smooth running of the school. My unease increased even further when I was presented with an engraved tankard - an ironic contrast with the receiving of nothing at all after nine years at John Rigby.

As I looked back on the previous eleven years I was able to review and, in some cases, to appreciate the significance of several changes in my life. I had started out unthinkingly as a luke-warm Conservative and ended up a committed Socialist, perceiving this ideology as the right complement to my Christian belief. I had discovered, too, the solid dependability and integrity of those who lived in a Lancashire town, and this had changed radically the value I placed upon people and how they should be treated. At the start of 1960 I was just a probationary teacher; by 1971 I had performed the roles of both a head of department and deputy head, albeit a resigned one. My customary mode of travel had graduated from simple public transport to executive performance car, and my sporting enthusiasm had moved from football to Rugby. Also, I was just a bit closer to becoming a confirmed bachelor.

I now had six weeks to prepare myself for Ruffwood School. This was not just a question of planning a curriculum, but the making of some sort of psychological preparation as well. The school was huge, but its size was mitigated by its warmth, and so there were positive points to consider. It did not take long for me to wonder why on earth I had selected the option of working with children displaying behaviour problems from the choices Alan Barnes had presented to me at that first meeting. For someone recovering from a major breakdown, it had the 'kill or cure' feel about it. Would I survive, or was I approaching the end of my chosen career? The answer to that, and to many other questions, follows in the third book.

124

St Richard's under-14 Football Team in 1971

The attractive wooded campus of Ruffwood School, Kirkby

For the first thirty-one years of my life, very little had gone wrong, aside from the death of my father when I was just thirteen. I had been happy at home and happy at school. I had achieved my objectives, as well as having what I had regarded then as the good fortune to miss National Service. I had applied successfully for two teaching posts, and a distant relative had bought me a car. I was fortunate to have a wide range of good friends. Then, I stepped into hell, subsequently understanding, as we all must, that it is through adversity that we learn most about who we really are. It is only through such experiences that the benefits of misfortune become clear: a deeper understanding of others; a deeper understanding of oneself. Yet we are not endowed with the ability to evaluate the present in retrospect. I return, then, to W H Auden's advice:

> Not even the first of the Romans can learn
> His Roman history in the future tense,
> Not even to serve your political turn;
> Hindsight as foresight makes no sense.

POSTSCRIPT

Some may question the advisability of recounting details of a breakdown in a book such as this. There are two reasons for including the episode: firstly, simply because it happened, and secondly, to provide an exposition for those who will have undergone a similar experience, and who will identify with some of the symptoms. It is generally believed that three quarters of the population will suffer acute anxiety at some point in their lives. The fortunate ones are those who survive it.

*

I list below what became of some of those in this book:

In 1972 the John Rigby Grammar School was redesignated as a mixed Sixth Form College, serving Catholic students on advanced courses.

The Hon. Mark Watson started an up-market antique business in Montpelier Terrace, off the Brompton Road in 1973, in partnership with his retired dentist friend, Ken. As the energy crisis damaged sales in the mid-1970s, the enterprise failed, and Mark moved from his lavish house in Brompton Square to an only slightly less prestigious property in Eaton Place. He died at the end of that decade.

After Brother Ambrose left John Rigby, he became Head of Scotus Academy in Edinburgh, later moving back to the north-west as Deputy Head of St Mary's College, Crosby. He died in 1997 and the funeral was held at St Peter & Paul in Crosby.

Kevin Sharkey died in 1992 after retiring from John Rigby. He remained a very close friend, and I shall ever be grateful for the consistent support he gave me during my illness.

126

Marie Sharkey was a highly-valued friend, both to me and to my mother. She was a committed Christian with many qualities, integrity being just one. Although her health was not good, she bore her difficulties with courage and dignity. Marie died in 2001.

Frank Balmer retired from teaching at John Rigby and, when he died, the funeral at St James, Orrell, drew an enormous number of mourners, many of them former pupils. Six Rugby players he had formerly coached acted as coffin bearers.

Brian Lewis became Head of the Art Department at John Rigby after I left, and remained at the School, and later the College, until he retired as Senior Teacher in 1990. He is now a successful sculptor.

Tony Hilton moved from John Rigby in 1970 to lecture at Christ's College in Liverpool. He taught for a year at Wigan Convent before returning to John Rigby College as Head of History in 1972, spending the remainder of his career there. He is currently working as an independent scholar, publishing historical books and journal papers.

John Mockett became Deputy Head of Campion School in St Helens in 1970, later becoming Headteacher. He lived in Bolton with his wife, Sheila. This man of considerable talent died in 1994.

Paula Velarde has followed the career of professional painter since leaving art college, teaching in schools and as a personal tutor. She married Mike Rudd and they live in Lower Dolphinholme near Lancaster.

Anne-Marie Meslin married Bernard Leclerq and has combined the role of mother to five children with that of schoolteacher. The family lives in Marcoing in northern France.

Brother O'Halloran moved from the headship of John Rigby, when it became a Sixth Form College in 1972, to become Head of St Mary's College in Crosby, where he was a colleague of Brother Ambrose. He has now retired to St Anselm's College, Birkenhead, where he was Head before coming to John Rigby.

Peter McLaughlin continued his career as Head of St Richard's, located in new premises in Tanhouse, until retirement. He was awarded the Bene Merenti Medal for services to education. I remember him as man of high quality, a fine mentor and, to me, something of a father-figure.

St Richard's High School, as it was later called, merged with St Thomas's in 1993 to form a single Catholic High School to serve the people of Skelmersdale.

The third book will deal with a few agonies and many ecstasies of teaching in Kirkby from 1971 to 1989, a six-week headship, two contrasting television appearances, a year in Cardiff on a Master's Degree, fifteen years of writing music, the fun of teaching French and a close encounter with a shark.

Memorabilia relating to 'The Diary of a Southport Man' @ £7.50

In addition to this book, there are two new video programmmes relating to the John Rigby Grammar School. Purchasing details are given below:

1 'THE FOOL ON THE HILL'
video programme @ £10.95 inc postage

This modern film dramatisation of the Stations of the Cross was made at John Rigby on Super 8mm cine in Spring 1968, and had now been transferred to video. Also on the cassette are an interview with Peter Hurst who played Christ, 'The Tell-Tale Heart', a horror story made in 1969, a re-enactment of 'The Fall of Harald Hardrada' made in 1970, and extracts from Rugby, Athletics and Cross-Country fixtures in 1963-4.

2 'JOHN RIGBY GRAMMAR SCHOOL REMEMBERED'
video programme @ £10.95 inc postage
available from December 2002

A large collection of camera interviews recording the anecdotes of former pupils and staff who were at John Rigby between 1959 and 1972, integrated with contemporary photographs, and producing an illuminating archive of the thirteen years the School existed before it became a college.

Memorabilia relating to 'The Diary of a Southport Boy' @ £7.50

This volume, covering the period 1937 to 1960, immediately precedes the current one. Associated items include the following:

3 'KGV REMEMBERED' video programme @ £10.95 inc post

The 81-minute programme about King George V School, Southport consists of over 60 interviews accompanied by more than 250 photographs.

4 'THE RED ROSE: STORIES OF KGV' @ £7.50 inc postage

This 160-page book contains memories, information and photographs from the opening of Southport Boys' Secondary School at 'The Woodlands' in 1920 to the closure of KGV in 1979, when it became a sixth form college.

Ordering

These and other items may be ordered from:

Artworks, 46 Lyndhurst Road, Southport PR8 4JT.   Tel: 01704 565075

e-mail: artworks @easicom.com   www.artworks-pictures.co.uk

Cheques should be made payable either to 'Artworks'
or, in the case of 3 and 4, to 'Old Georgians'